The
Predator ACTD

A Case Study for
Transition Planning
to the
Formal Acquisition Process

Michael R. Thirtle • Robert V. Johnson • John L. Birkler

Prepared for the
Office of the Secretary of Defense

National Defense Research Institute

RAND

In July 1995, a new endurance unmanned aerial vehicle (UAV) flew over Bosnia to surveil and provide all-weather reconnaissance and image-gathering in an operational (i.e., conflict) environment. Representing a new capability for the Department of Defense (DoD), this UAV represented, above all, a departure from DoD's usual way of doing acquisition business. The study documented in this report was completed in support of RAND research on Advanced Concept Technology Demonstration (ACTD) programs for the Office of the Secretary of Defense. The effort was conducted from July until December 1996 and documents research on the Medium Altitude Endurance (MAE) Unmanned Aerial Vehicle ACTD program, also known as the Predator UAV.

Specifically, RAND was tasked to examine two questions: (1) What were the overarching lessons learned from the Predator ACTD? and (2) Which lessons can be generalized and applied to other ACTD programs? In this analysis, we closely detail the Predator ACTD and also document the important demonstration and transition issues from the project that can be applied to other ACTDs. The intent of this work is to improve the ACTD process and the transition of ACTDs to formal acquisition programs. This report should be of interest to those involved in acquisition, program offices, and ACTD programs.

The research for this report was performed in the Acquisition and Technology Policy Center of RAND's National Defense Research

Institute, a federally funded research and development center supported by the Office of the Secretary of Defense, the Joint Staff, and the defense agencies.

CONTENTS

FIGURES

TABLES

INTRODUCTION

In July 1995, a new endurance unmanned aerial vehicle, the Predator, flew over Bosnia to surveil and provide all-weather reconnaissance and image-gathering in an operational (i.e., conflict) environment. It represented not only a new capability for the Department of Defense (DoD) but a departure from DoD's usual way of doing acquisition business.

As the military has been faced with significant constraints on its ability to procure weapon systems during the past decade, the acquisition community has experienced great change. To maintain a robust posture in the face of reductions in procurement funding, the DoD has endeavored to increase both the effectiveness and efficiency of the existing acquisition framework. Recent examples include the use of streamlined business processes, process improvement teams, and the Advanced Concept Technology Demonstration (ACTD). The idea for ACTDs was generated by senior DoD leaders in 1993 because they perceived that the formal acquisition process was inefficient in demonstrating new technology to warfighters.

ACTDs represent an integrated effort to assemble and demonstrate a significant, novel, and improved military capability that is based on mature, advanced technologies. Whereas, historically, developing new capabilities has taken a decade or even longer, the ACTD process, from start to finish, is intended to take no more than three years. Within this short schedule, project sizes are scaled so that operational utility, or military utility, and system integrity can be established quickly.

An ACTD is a *joint exercise:* It is developed and implemented by both the operational user and the materiel development communities. Acceptance or rejection of an ACTD is based on the warfighter's evaluation of the military utility of the system as well as on other factors, such as affordability and supportability.

Given these criteria, not all ACTDs are expected to be successful or to make the transition to the formal acquisition process. During the time frame when the ACTD process was initially being formulated, an existing project—the Medium Altitude Endurance (MAE) Unmanned Aerial Vehicle (UAV), or Predator, a new system within the 50-year-old UAV family—was selected to serve as one of the prototypes for testing the ACTD concept. The Predator was one of the first ACTDs to be completed and also to make the transition to the formal acquisition process. It therefore provides a unique opportunity to study the ACTD process for issues and lessons learned, so that defense acquisition and management methods can be improved.

Along with the fast pace of ACTDs, the lack of formal acquisition rules, DoD's inexperience with the ACTD process, and the limited operational capability of the prototypes, issues abounded on how to conduct and make successful transition to the formal acquisition process. The purpose of the research documented here was to conduct a case-study analysis of the prototype Predator ACTD and to capture lessons learned (both positive and negative) that can be applied to other ACTDs. The main challenge in this process was to divine which lessons were unique to the Predator and which could be generalized.

MILITARY UTILITY

Of the many aspects that differentiate an ACTD from a formal acquisition program, perhaps the most significant is the role that military utility plays in the overall process. Whereas formal acquisition programs have traditionally involved operational users during various milestones throughout a program's life cycle, the ACTD process increases the fidelity of such involvement to the point that an ACTD may continue or fold according to the customer's assessment of the technology's worth.

By an ACTD's definition, operational users not only participate in the management and execution of program decisions, they also provide the final decision on whether an ACTD should be transitioned to the formal acquisition process. If warfighters believe that an ACTD has military value, then "military utility" is declared and the ACTD is transitioned, provided that ample funding exists. If utility is not declared, an ACTD may possibly never be transitioned or technologies derived from the ACTD process may be shelved for later use and make the transition as individual elements. In any case, relative to formal acquisition programs, the declaration of military utility represents a unique and marked change by shifting responsibility from developer to operational warfighter.

THE CONTEXT FOR THE PREDATOR ACTD

Since the end of World War II, the DoD has managed several UAV programs. UAVs have a better fit in today's military than they had during the preceding 50 years. The advent of enhanced satellite communications, radar imagery, and stand-off capabilities has forced many military planners to rethink the role UAVs can play in the battle environment—possibly even replacing certain types of manned aircraft. The importance of and, likewise, interest in the UAV family of systems has grown steadily since the 1980s, when the first UAV Master Plan was developed by the UAV Joint Program Office. The master plan provides the centerpiece for both strategic vision and implementation aspects of UAV programs within the DoD. As the technical aspects of UAV programs have evolved during the past decade, so has the UAV Joint Program Office's (JPO's) vision for structuring the UAV family. Today, within the parameters of the endurance group of aerial vehicles, there are three tiers of UAVs. Each is focused upon a unique duration and altitude, and each encompasses correspondingly different system requirements.

As the UAV JPO was finishing the planning of the tiered concept in 1993, the DoD sought out potential bidders for the development of Tier II, also known as the Medium Altitude Endurance (MAE) UAV. Specifically, the Under Secretary of Defense for Acquisition called for a new UAV system that required greater endurance capabilities—this request was known among members of the UAV community as the "Deutch Memo."[1] Although the Gnat-750 UAV existed at the time of the development request, policymakers decided that it could not adequately perform the types of missions that would be demanded of the system. Key specifications of the UAV included an ability to fly 500 nautical miles, remain on station over a target for at least 24 hours, lift a 400–500-pound payload, and fly at altitudes of 15,000–25,000 feet. Instead, a new system, called the Predator UAV, was developed and produced to fill the Tier II UAV niche.

As initial discussions of the Predator UAV concept began to solidify into a documented business plan, the DoD was in the process of finalizing the strategy for implementing the ACTD process. In April 1994, a list of the first six candidate ACTDs—the Predator UAV was among them—was released to the public. Like its ACTD counterparts, the demonstration of the Predator UAV focused on three criteria: the demonstration of a mature technology that did not require significant development, a focus on displaying the system in an operational environment, and the successful execution of the program itself. The Predator UAV ACTD achieved all three of these prior to its eventual transition to the formal acquisition process.

PROGRAM DESCRIPTION

The Deutch Memo initiated the development of the Predator UAV to fill the Tier II operational need. In total, the ACTD lasted 30 months from 1994 through 1996 and comprised several operational assessments, including use of the Predator in Bosnia to support U.S. and NATO surveillance needs. Predator was also used in training exercises such as DoD's Roving Sands in the desert of New Mexico, U.S. Customs Service's drug-enforcement activities, and the U.S. Navy's Commander in Chief of the Pacific Fleet (CINCPACFLT) Composite Training Unit Exercise (COMPTUEX) 96-1A. Performance feedback during the various exercises facilitated the inclusion of several technical changes to the Predator UAV. Examples of changes included improved radar and de-icing capabilities. This hallmark of

---

[1] Under Secretary of Defense John M. Deutch, "Endurance Unmanned Aerial Vehicle (UAV) Program," memo to the Assistant Secretary of the Navy for Research, Development & Acquisition, July 12, 1993.

the ACTD process—demand for real-time feedback—enabled the technical aspects of the Predator UAV to mature as more iterations were accomplished. Relative to the formal acquisition process, which relies upon developmental and operational testing to gain similar feedback, the ACTD used in actual exercises and military operations to conduct its assessments of the Predator UAV system.

To analyze the efficiency and effectiveness of the business aspects of the Predator UAV ACTD, we used several standard functional categories that should be well known to professionals who are familiar with the formal acquisition process. In all, we studied the Predator UAV with respect to seven areas: management methods, communication techniques, operational requirements, testing methodology, procurement strategy, financial management, and system supportability. Because these functions are common to both ACTDs and formal acquisition programs, their contrast brings obvious disparities into sharp relief. For example, we observed that ACTD program managers must have a well-constructed plan for communicating within the organization—no different from what is needed in the formal acquisition process to ensure a successful program completion. An example that highlights the stark difference between the two processes is that the Predator ACTD utilized minimal supportability documentation, whereas a typical formal acquisition program tends to require a significant amount of supportability data and reference documents. Although these two examples highlight the similarities and differences between ACTDs and formal acquisition programs, we discovered several others throughout the analysis as well; these are highlighted in the body of the report and are summarized in tabular form.

ISSUES FRAMEWORK

We identified two general types of issues during our analysis of the Predator UAV ACTD by the seven criteria listed above: demonstration issues, which capture lessons from the ACTD's operational exercises, and transition issues, which capture aspects that must be dealt with as the ACTD proceeds to the formal acquisition process. Tables S.1 and S.2 highlight the major demonstration and transition

Table S.1

Demonstration Issues

Subject	Issues
Choice of demonstration and operational managers	• Skills base • Mutual relationship
Characteristics of the government program office	• Size of organization • Use of Memoranda of Agreement to create a virtual organization • Selection of personnel with experience
Measures of program control	• Emphasis on informal communications • Contract Data Requirements List items
Selection of lead service	• Timing of decision • Methodology of choice
Declaration of military utility	• Timing in relation to selection of lead service • Qualitative or quantitative methodology
Stability of funding	• Funding considerations throughout ACTD
Personnel requirements	• Service commitment • Uniformity of skills • Training
Involvement of Operational Test Agencies (OTAs)	• Timing of involvement • Benefits of operational testing

issues that we observed and discuss here in relation to the Predator ACTD.

Although the issues presented in these tables were discovered through analyzing the Predator UAV ACTD, all can be generalized and applied to other types of ACTDs as well. After identifying the issues listed above, we provide recommendations on how future ACTDs may benefit from the Predator experience. For example, with regard to the minimal supportability documentation noted above, although acquisition-reform principles in the formal acquisition process have encouraged typical programs to reduce logistics data requirements as well, the Predator ACTD clearly did not order enough to achieve its goals. In fact, problems such as a lack of training documentation and a heavy reliance upon contractor support were identified as potential pitfalls within the ACTD. A recommendation for other ACTDs is to consider the use of logistics and supportability

Table S.2

ACTD Transition Issues

Subject	Issues
Supportability	• Need for planning • Operational user involvement • Technical orders and data • Residual support
Producibility	• Effect on initial source selection
Program oversight	• OSD involvement • Type of management organization
Funding and affordability	• POM wedge for follow-on work • Need for life-cycle-cost estimate
Operational Requirements Document (ORD)	• Development of a draft ORD • Inclusion of reliability and maintainability goals
Test planning	• Development of an initial Developmental Test and Evaluation (DT&E) plan • Documenting feedback from operational assessments

information that not only can be used during the demonstration of the ACTD but that may be analyzed for technical and performance trade-offs as the system matures.

CONCLUSIONS AND RECOMMENDATIONS

Through interviews we conducted with both government and contractor personnel within the Predator program, we were able to synthesize a list of concepts that were critical to the success of that program. Likewise, we examined several other ideas that the program did not use but that we believe could prove to be of great benefit for other ACTDs as well. Table S.3 summarizes some of those recommendations.

For the most part, methods for managing ACTDs are new within the DoD and represent a major cultural change to developing and demonstrating systems in the formal acquisition process. Until recently, business operations in the acquisition environment had centered around life-cycle acquisition and support. Consequently, most

Table S.3

Results of Analysis of the Predator ACTD

- Given the necessarily fast pace of the ACTD process, confident, effective, and innovative individuals are critical to the success of a program.

- The lead service must be selected early in the ACTD process to ensure that (1) proper test and logistics planning occurs, (2) operational requirements are fleshed out, and (3) warfighters have complete buy-in to the system—participating in the ACTD from start to finish and being stakeholders in the product (not just observers)—to ensure its longevity and success.

- An ACTD needs to be managed significantly differently than are formal acquisition programs, because of the (1) fast-paced program schedule, (2) small number of program office personnel, and (3) limited guidance on how to perform the acquisition of the system.

- Test agencies such as the Defense Evaluation Support Activity (DESA) and the Air Force Operational Test and Evaluation Center (AFOTEC) made beneficial inputs; their involvement should be considered with future ACTDs.

- The lead-service organization should develop a draft Operational Requirements Document during the ACTD process. The process of writing and constantly updating the ORD will (1) resolve any misunderstanding of requirements among developers and warfighters, (2) help define quantitative system specifications, and (3) facilitate transition of the ACTD to the acquisition process.

- ACTDs should consider more in-depth planning than they do now, and it should occur earlier in their schedule than was done for the Predator. Planning discussions must involve operational users, lead-service personnel, and acquisition experts who can assess functional areas such as test, logistics, engineering, and affordability. Such planning is especially important if a strong probability exists that the ACTD will make the transition to the formal acquisition process upon its completion.

individuals within the acquisition system are accustomed to using the following DoD 5000 methods for managing programs: (1) avoidance of past mistakes, (2) a focus on risk mitigation, and (3) a strict adherence to formal processes. In the past several years, however, revisions to DoD 5000 Series have facilitated streamlining and have encouraged people to think about more-creative and more-effective solutions to problems.[2] Acquisition-reform initiatives have con-

---

[2]See especially U.S. Department of Defense, *Defense Acquisition*, DODD 5000.1, March 15, 1996, and *Mandatory Procedures for Major Defense Acquisition Programs (MDAPs)*

centrated on improving processes to procure systems faster, more cost-effectively, and with the use of more-commercial practices and commercial off-the-shelf (COTS) items. Although of great long-term benefit to the DoD, these changes have not been easy to implement culturally by policymakers because of the paradigms held by stakeholders of the formal acquisition process, which relies on three key variables: (1) the depth of planning accomplished, (2) the formality of processes, and (3) the amount of documentation required.

This report contains findings and lessons learned that recognize the eventual connectivity between ACTDs and DoD 5000 requirements. Many of the lessons indicate a need for more planning, closer co-ordination among participants, and greater resources; however, this is not to say that the methods for managing ACTD programs *should* evolve in scope or detail as do those associated with DoD 5000 programs. On the contrary, the utility of the ACTD process lies in its ability to demonstrate technologies to operational users expediently.

We expect that recommendations from this study will aid in making the ACTD process a more effective and efficient one by recognizing that every ACTD is unique and that content must be tailored to best fit the objectives of the program.

---

and Major Automated Information System (MAIS) Acquisition Programs, DoD Regulation 5000.2-R, December 13, 1996.

ACKNOWLEDGMENTS

We would like to thank Tom Perdue, Principal Assistant Deputy Under Secretary of Defense (Advanced Technology), and John Smith, Deputy Director, Acquisition Program Integration, Office of the Under Secretary of Defense (Acquisition and Technology), for their guidance, suggestions, and forthright comments. Many other organizations were also cooperative and gave us their time, program data, and information to assist in this effort. These included the personnel of the Program Executive Officer for Cruise Missile and Unmanned Aerial Vehicles [(PEO)CU]; the MAE UAV Demonstration Manager; the MAE UAV Operational Manager in the United States Atlantic Command; the Air Combat Command; the Defense Airborne Reconnaissance Office; the United States Air Force Operational Test and Evaluation Command; the Defense Evaluation Support Activity; and the General Atomics Aeronautical Systems, Inc., contractor team. Without their willing support, we could not have succeeded in capturing the lessons learned from the program. We also extend our deepest gratitude to Marian Branch, who improved the structure and clarity of the report. RAND colleagues Elliot Axelband and Jeffrey Drezner provided constructive and insightful technical reviews of an earlier draft of the study. Any errors included in this report are, of course, solely our responsibility.

ACC	Air Combat Command
ACTD	Advanced Concept Technology Demonstration
AFB	Air Force Base
AFMC	Air Force Materiel Command
AFOTEC	Air Force Operational Test and Evaluation Center
AGL	above ground level
AJP	Advanced Joint Planning
ASN(RD&A)	Assistant Secretary of the Navy (Research, Development and Acquisition)
ATO	air tasking order
BADD	Battlefield Awareness and Data Dissemination
BMDO	Ballistic Missile Defense Organization
BPI	Boost Phase Intercept
C/SCSC	Cost/Schedule Control System Criteria
C3I	Command, Control, Communications, and Intelligence
C4I	Command, Control, Communications, Computers, and Intelligence
CAIV	Cost As an Independent Variable
CDR	Critical Design Review
CDRL	Contract Data Requirements List
CECOM	Communications/Electronics Command
CIA	Central Intelligence Agency
CINC	Commander in Chief
CINCLANTFLT	Commander in Chief of the Atlantic Fleet
CINCPACFLT	Commander in Chief of the Pacific Fleet

CLS	Contractor Logistics Support
COI	Critical Operational Issues
COMPTUEX	Composite Training Unit Exercise (Navy)
COMSAT	communications satellite
CONOPS	concept of operations
CONUS	continental United States
CONV	Conventional (UAV)
COTS	Commercial Off-the-Shelf (equipment or components)
CP	Counterproliferation
CR	Close Range (UAV)
CY	calendar year
DAE	Defense Acquisition Executive
DAMO-FDZ	Office of the Director of Force Development, Deputy Chief of Staff for Operations and Plans, Department of the Army
DARO	Defense Airborne Reconnaissance Office
DARPA	Defense Advanced Research Projects Agency
DAWIA	Defense Activities Workforce Improvement Act
DDM	Deputy Demonstration Manager
DESA	Defense Evaluation Support Activity
DM	Demonstration Manager
DoD	Department of Defense
DODD	Department of Defense Directive
DOE	Department of Energy
DSB	Defense Science Board
DSWA	Defense Special Weapons Agency
DT	Developmental Test
DT&E	Developmental Test and Evaluation
DUSD/AT	Deputy Under Secretary of Defense, Advanced Technology
EMD	Engineering and Manufacturing Development
EO	electro-optical
FAR	Federal Acquisition Regulation
FORSCOM	U.S. Army Forces Command
FY	fiscal year
GA-ASI	General Atomics Aeronautical Systems, Inc.

GCS	ground control station
GPS	Global Positioning System
HAE	High Altitude Endurance (UAV)
HALE	High Altitude Long Endurance (UAV)
IARS	Integrated Airborne Reconnaissance Strategy
IFF	Identification Friend or Foe
IFOR	Implementation Force
IMINT	image intelligence
INS	Inertial Navigation System
IOT&E	Initial Operation Test and Evaluation
IR	Infrared
JCS	Joint Chiefs of Staff
JFACC	Joint Force Air Component Commander
JFC	Joint Force Commander
JIC	Joint Intelligence Center
JPO	Joint Program Office
JROC	Joint Requirements Oversight Council
JTF	Joint Task Force
JT TAC	Joint Tactical UAV
JWCA	Joint Warfare Capability Assessment
KIAS	knots indicated airspeed
LCC	life-cycle cost
LO	low observable
LOS	line of sight
LSA	Logistics Support Analysis
LRU	line-replaceable unit
MAE	Medium Altitude Endurance (UAV)
MNS	Mission Needs Statement
MOA	Memorandum of Agreement
MOE	measure of effectiveness
MOP	measure of performance
MR	Medium Range (UAV)
MRL	multiple rocket launcher
MTBF	mean time between failure
NASA	National Aeronautics and Space Administration
NATO	North Atlantic Treaty Organization
NAVAIR	Naval Air Systems Command

NIIRS	National Imagery Interpretability Rating Scale
OA	Operational Assessment
OM	Operational Manager
ORD	Operational Requirements Document
OSD	Office of the Secretary of Defense
OT&E	Operational Test and Evaluation
OTA	Operational Test Agency
OTL	Ordnance Test Laboratory
PDR	Preliminary Design Review
PEO	Program Executive Officer
PEO(CU)	Program Executive Officer for Cruise Missiles and Unmanned Aerial Vehicles
PLSS	Precision Locator Strike System
PM	program manager
POM	Program Objective Memorandum
PPBS	Planning, Programming, and Budgeting System
RPV	Remotely Piloted Vehicle
RS	remote site
SAE	Service Acquisition Executive
SAR	Synthetic Aperture Radar
SATCOM	satellite communications
SIGINT	signals intelligence
SM	System Manager
SME	Subject Matter Expert
SPO	System Program Office
SR	Short Range (UAV)
SR-B1	Short Range Block One (UAV)
SRU	shop-replaceable unit
SSN	nuclear-powered submarine
STOW	Synthetic Theater of War
TAC	Tactical (UAV)
TDY	temporary duty
TEMP	Test and Evaluation Master Plan
TIPT	Transition Integrated Product Team
TRA	Teledyne Ryan Aeronautical
TSII	Trojan Spirit II System
UAV	unmanned aerial vehicle

UHF	ultra-high frequency
UN	United Nations
USA	United States Army
USACOM	United States Atlantic Command
USAF	United States Air Force
USCENTCOM	United States Central Command
USCS	United States Customs Service
USD(A&T)	Under Secretary of Defense, Acquisition and Technology
USEUCOM	United States European Command
USMC	United States Marine Corps
USN	United States Navy
USSOCOM	United States Special Operations Command
VCJCS	Vice Chairman of the Joint Chiefs of Staff
VLC	Very Low Cost (UAV)
WBS	Work Breakdown Structure
WG	Working Group

Chapter One

INTRODUCTION

In July 1995, a new endurance unmanned aerial vehicle (UAV) flew over Bosnia to surveil and provide all-weather reconnaissance and image-gathering in an operational (i.e., conflict) environment. Representing a new capability for the Department of Defense (DoD) that both extended the pedigree on an already-extensive line of UAVs and realized a concept within 30 months, it represented, above all, a departure from DoD's usual way of doing acquisition business. This report is about that line, that UAV, and, above all, that departure—the Advanced Concept Technology Demonstration.

BACKGROUND

During the past three years (1994–1996), the DoD has placed special emphasis upon incorporating the viewpoints of *operational users*, or warfighters, into the acquisition process. Although varying amounts of customer inputs have been considered throughout the history of the formal acquisition process, many military and civilian leaders have thought that the existing procurement system did not provide enough flexibility or fungibility for quick demonstration of capability. In 1993, an idea was conceived by senior DoD leadership—the Advanced Concept Technology Demonstration (ACTD) process—to directly address the early stages of the acquisition process. One year later, an implementation plan was formalized.

Essentially a quick-look demonstration (typically two to four years) of the operational capability of low-risk, mature technologies not previously examined by the complete acquisition process, an ACTD focuses on the operational user and is expected to perform in operational settings to demonstrate military utility. The development of formal requirement documentation is not mandatory.

According to current guidance from the Office of the Secretary of Defense (OSD), completion of the ACTD project should result in one of three scenarios:

- The project could end and be cancelled.

- The project could be shelved for later use.

- The project could make the transition into the formal acquisition process.

In any of the three cases, one tangible outcome of the ACTD is the production of residual assets: "leftovers" from the ACTD that can be used in the operational environment. Acceptance or rejection of a system is based on the user's evaluation of the utility of the system, as well as on other factors such as affordability and supportability.

Around the same time that the ACTD process was formulated, an existing program was selected to serve as one of the prototypes for testing the process. This program, the Medium Altitude Endurance (MAE) Unmanned Aerial Vehicle, or Predator, was a new system within the UAV family and represents a significant milestone in the continuing process of military acquisition reform.

OBJECTIVES AND APPROACH OF THIS STUDY

Besides being the first ACTD to be initiated, Predator was also the first to make the transition into the formal acquisition process.[1] Both of these facts mark the study of the Predator ACTD as a beneficial and likewise necessary exercise for disseminating information on issues of acquisition reform. And for these same reasons, this study focuses on capturing the lessons learned from the Predator experience and on describing how they can be applied to other ACTDs. The following were the main questions that arose in our analysis and represent our key objectives:

---

[1]We provide a more detailed discussion of the ACTD process and types of ACTDs in Chapter Two.

- What are the history and components of the ACTD process?

- How was the Predator program implemented as an ACTD?

- What organizations were involved in managing the Predator?

- What were the unique characteristics of the Predator ACTD?

- What are the lessons to be learned from the Predator experience as the first ACTD to be initiated, as well as the first to make the transition into the formal acquisition process?

- Which issues can be generalized and applied to other ACTD programs for their successful management and transition?

To meet these objectives, we employed several methods for collecting and analyzing information: interviewing key government and contractor personnel, reviewing historical documentation, consulting with RAND colleagues, and attending meetings related to the ACTD process.

Interviews of key players within the Predator program were critical to ensuring a complete representation of the issues. We talked with stakeholders with differing perspectives on the program: government personnel of the Office of the Deputy Under Secretary of Defense, Advanced Technology (DUSD/AT), the Defense Airborne Reconnaissance Office (DARO), the Program Executive Officer for Cruise Missiles and Unmanned Aerial Vehicles [PEO(CU)], the Predator UAV Demonstration Manager (DM), the U.S. Atlantic Command (USACOM) Operational Manager (OM), the U.S. Air Force (USAF) Air Combat Command (ACC), the USAF Operational Test and Evaluation Center (AFOTEC), and the Defense Evaluation Support Activity (DESA); and the management team of the prime contractor, General Atomics Aeronautical Systems, Inc. (GA-ASI).

ORGANIZATION OF THE REPORT

This report documents our interpretation of the process that the Predator ACTD followed. It uses the qualifiers for the definition of *Advanced Concept Technology Demonstration* to frame specific contexts for the Predator in relation to the development of unmanned aerial vehicles in general and the tiered approach to developing specific UAVs, and the reason for its selection as an ACTD; it provides an overview of the Predator ACTD program itself to establish the components of both the development and demonstration of the vehicle and the business and management characteristics of the program that link it with acquisition programs and set it apart from them; it then reexamines those components by identifying two general categories of issues arising from the program—demonstration issues and transition issues—and recommends procedures for dealing with those issues. It concludes by presenting the major recommendations we derived from our analysis.

Chapter Two provides a broad context, giving information about the ACTD process and the ancestry of the Predator UAV, which establishes it as a new concept within a framework of mature technology. Chapter Two also provides information on the UAV Joint Program Office (JPO), the development of the tiered approach to UAV management, and a discussion of the three classes of ACTDs. Chapter Three describes the Predator ACTD itself: (1) its origins as a separate and distinct UAV and an overview of the program and (2) business and management aspects of the program. The chapter also includes a framework comprising essential elements of the program that figure largely in formal DoD acquisition processes. Chapter Four builds on this framework by discussing the two types of major issues observed throughout our analysis of the Predator ACTD: (1) those facilitating better program execution for the duration of an ACTD and (2) those creating an effective transition into the formal acquisition process. This chapter also summarizes the similarities and differences between the Predator ACTD and a formal acquisition program. Lastly, in Chapter Five, we provide conclusions that pertain to future ACTDs.

A NOTE ON MILITARY UTILITY

Military utility is the heart and soul of an ACTD—its defining characteristic, in fact. We keep referring to it throughout this report because it represents a significant departure from the formal acquisition process, for which there is no such defining characteristic. Without its focus on military utility, the entire ACTD process would cease to exist.

Chapter Two

THE HISTORICAL CONTEXT FOR THE PREDATOR ACTD

Like the formal acquisition process, the business of ACTDs is a complex one. Full appreciation of the types of policy issues that were raised, as well as the methods implemented during the ACTD process, requires a thorough understanding of the context for those issues. It is our contention that the context for the Predator UAV can best be illustrated by describing historical information about UAVs, discussing the specifications for the Medium Altitude Endurance (MAE) system, and delineating the ACTD process from which the Predator was demonstrated.

AN ABBREVIATED HISTORY OF UAVs

The United States has been involved with developing UAVs and target drones since shortly after the end of World War II. During the past 50 years, the DoD has managed and used several UAV programs. In this section, we focus on those systems having a direct technical relationship to the Predator UAV system. Our goal here is not to provide a complete analysis of all UAVs during the past five decades but, rather, to discuss the highlights of a few key programs as a means of establishing a context in which to analyze the Predator ACTD.

The Demand for UAVs

As evidenced by recent examples of U.S. intervention in military conflicts such as Bosnia and Southwest Asia, the United States' stake in an unmanned surveillance and imaging system—a UAV system—

has increased significantly during the past few years. This is not to say that UAVs were not of value during other periods, but the advent of enhanced satellite communications, radar imagery, and stand-off capabilities has forced many military planners to rethink the role UAVs can play in the battle environment. According to recent projections, the UAV market could grow by approximately 10–15 percent during the next six years, from current expenditure levels of $350 million in 1996 to projected levels of approximately $400 million by 2002.[1] Correlated with the increased interest in the UAV concept, another important development during the past few years has been the change in the attitudes of military leadership toward using such vehicles in the operational environment. For the first time in the contemporary history of the Air Force, the Chief of Staff of the USAF indicated in 1996 that pilotless vehicles will play significant roles in the future battlespace environment—even possibly replacing certain types of manned aircraft.[2] These trends suggest that UAV systems such as the Predator will be highly sought after in the future.

The UAV Joint Program Office (JPO) and Its Master Plan

In response to what was deemed the ineffectiveness of previous U.S. UAV development and acquisition efforts during the early 1980s, Congress directed two important changes for the restructuring of DoD UAV programs: (1) that the DoD consolidate all nonlethal, nonweapon UAV programs within the U.S. Armed Forces into one joint program office and (2) that the JPO prepare an annual UAV Master Plan detailing prospective UAV development and acquisition strategies. Both changes resulted directly in the establishment of the UAV JPO to facilitate the development and deployment of UAVs efficiently and effectively. Today, the JPO is located within the PEO(CU) and has coordination and decisionmaking authority over all nonlethal UAVs being developed by the USAF, U.S. Army (USA), U.S. Marine Corps (USMC), U.S. Navy (USN), Defense Advanced Research Projects Agency (DARPA), and the OSD.

---

[1] *Air Force Times*, August 26, 1996.

[2] *Aerospace Daily*, July 21, 1995, pp. 102–104.

The first UAV Master Plan, produced by the JPO in 1988, included six projects: the Very Low Cost (VLC) UAV, the Close Range (CR) UAV, the Short Range (SR) UAV, the Short Range Block I (SR-B1) UAV, the Medium Range (MR) UAV, and the High-Altitude Long Endurance (HALE) UAV. By September 1992, the UAV Master Plan included the same six UAVs, but had essentially realigned them with a different category structure. Although Congress directed the DoD during 1991 to give the endurance UAV category the lowest system-development priority until the CR, SR, and MR systems could move closer to production, it appeared that the JPO was in the process of defining requirements for the endurance family of UAVs anyway.[3] Review of the 1993 UAV Master Plan indicated that the endurance program had indeed flourished while other programs were being reorganized.

Endurance UAVs: Lineage of the Predator

American endurance UAVs, such as the Predator, can trace their lineage to the Vietnam War, where the Compass Arrow UAV was introduced as one of the first American unmanned aerial vehicles to perform reconnaissance missions. The original mission of Compass Arrow was to conduct high-altitude flights; however, after a rewinging of the original version of the UAV in the 1960s, it was also able to perform longer—*endurance*—flights of up to 24 hours. The program remained in the DoD inventory until 1973.

One year prior to the storage of the Compass Arrow, the Compass Cope project was initiated as a joint program, sponsored by the Air Force and the National Security Agency. Development contracts for the program were given to Teledyne Ryan and Boeing, mainly for creating a UAV that would replace the U-2 spy plane and that could stay aloft for longer times than the Compass Arrow: Initial expectations were for 30 hours. Although Boeing was later selected as the sole-source contractor for system production, the program was eventually cancelled in 1977, before any extensive production had begun.

---

[3]J. Terino, "UAVs: A Defense Growth Area," *National Defense*, October 1992, pp. 13–14.

During the 1980s, the market for smaller, tactical UAVs began to flourish, as evidenced by the increase in the number of programs under development.[4] Systems developed during this time include the Pioneer, the Teal Rain, the Amber, the Condor, and the Aquila. Negative outcomes associated with the Aquila program, such as cost overruns and program schedule delays, provided a stimulus for the DoD to restructure its UAV program hierarchy by establishing a multitiered approach within the UAV Master Plan (the tiered approach is described in the following subsection).

Another significant product of the 1980s was a UAV called the Gnat-750, the direct predecessor to the Predator UAV. Produced by General Atomics Aeronautical Systems, Inc., of San Diego, California, the system was developed from technical concepts established under the Amber UAV program. The Gnat-750 has the capability of over 40 hours' endurance, has a wingspan of 35 feet, is 18 feet long, and has been used at altitudes of up to 25,000 feet. It has carried payloads of 140 pounds and has an overall weight (empty) of 1,140 pounds. As of July 1996, the Gnat-750 had accomplished five combat deployments, had participated in operations with Turkish forces, and had operated from 14 sites worldwide. The UAV has been used by the National Aeronautics and Space Administration (NASA), the Department of Energy (DOE), and the Central Intelligence Agency (CIA). It was the first UAV deployed to the Bosnia theater of operations.[5] The Gnat-750 also served the role of a Tier I UAV platform within the DoD UAV Master Plan.[6]

The Predator UAV evolved from the design of the Gnat-750 and was designated the Medium Altitude Endurance (MAE) UAV. Also developed by GA-ASI, the Predator system has a similar aerodynamic design to the Gnat's and includes an expanded electro-optical/infrared payload, a synthetic aperture radar (SAR), a data link by way of satellite communications, and the use of an inertial navigation system (INS) for directional control. The Predator has documented

---

[4]G. Sommer et al., *The Global Hawk Unmanned Aerial Vehicle Acquisition Process: A Summary of Phase 1 Experience,* Santa Monica, Calif.: RAND, MR-809-DARPA, 1997.

[5]GA-ASI Homepage, http://www.ga.com/, November 1996.

[6]U.S. Department of Defense, *Unmanned Aerial Vehicle 1994 Master Plan,* Washington, D.C., May 1994.

flight times longer than 40 hours and has flown at altitudes exceeding 25,000 feet. It measures approximately 48 feet wide by 28 feet long and can travel at speeds up to 120 knots.[7] The Predator can carry a larger payload than the Gnat-750's (450 pounds versus 140 pounds) and is a heavier vehicle (1,873 pounds versus 1,140 pounds).

Development of the Tiered Approach to Managing UAV Development

Shortly after the release of the 1993 Master Plan, the Joint Requirements Oversight Council (JROC) eliminated the requirement to buy medium-range UAVs for the Navy and Marine Corps—an action that seriously set back the UAV JPO's plans for procurement of the MR UAV, eventually leading to its outright cancellation. The remaining programs were reorganized into two groups: the Joint Tactical (JT TAC) UAV program (absorbing the CR UAV and the SR UAV) and the Endurance program. Elements of this newly formed three-tiered approach included (1) the Tier I UAV, a relatively small UAV with 24–30-hour endurance (the Gnat-750 served this role), (2) the Tier II UAV (the Predator) with 44-hour endurance, and (3) the Tier III UAV, which was envisioned as a large, ultra-long-range stealth UAV. Figure 2.1 shows the pedigree of the Tier concept, with an emphasis on the evolution of various UAV programs.[8]

Interestingly enough, the Gnat-750 program already existed when the decision was made to establish the tiered UAV management plan. Thus, it was apparent from the system's operational performance that it could fulfill the Tier I role as defined. The Tier II program, however, did not have a definite candidate. As early as 1988, it was reported that GA-ASI had been performing development studies of a growth version of the Gnat-750 that could fill the Tier II void, even though requirements for such a system were not announced until 1993. It seemed that GA-ASI had already been developing the Predator in anticipation of an enhanced endurance requirement and was actively marketing it at air and space trade shows.[9]

---

[7]GA-ASI Homepage, http://www.ga.com/, November 1996.

[8]For a more detailed discussion, see Sommer et al., 1997, pp. 10–13.

[9]*Forecast International/DMS Market Intelligence Report,* December 1991, p. 25.

RAND*MR899-2.1*

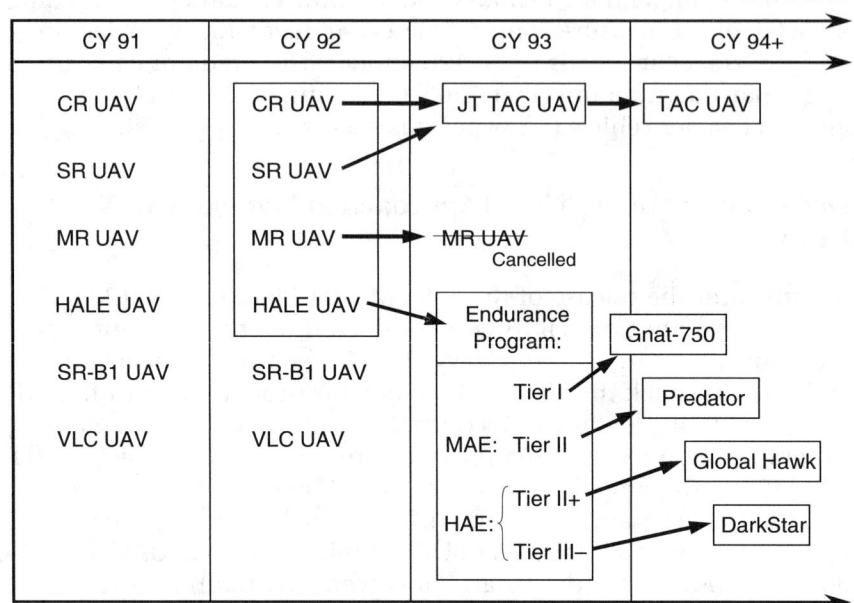

Figure 2.1—Pedigree of the Tier Concept

OVERVIEW OF THE MAE PROGRAM: HOW IT FILLED THE TIER II ROLE

As part of the Tier II approach, the DoD developed initial requirements to satisfy the need for a Medium Altitude Endurance vehicle.
This section describes the events leading up to the decision for the
Predator to fill that role, system specifications of the UAV, and a
description of its role in operational activities. As in the preceding
section, this description is not intended to provide a full account of
every single event and action but, rather, to enhance the reader's understanding of the Predator in the further analysis in Chapter Three.

Requirements for the MAE

Although JROC recommendations in May 1993 had roughly defined
the MAE requirements, the Under Secretary of Defense for Acquisi-

tion wrote a memo, in July 1993, to the Assistant Secretary of the Navy for Research, Development and Acquisition, refining the requirements of the system. The memo called for development of an MAE UAV that could accomplish the following:[10]

- Fly 500 nautical miles

- Stay on station for at least 24 hours

- Lift a 400–500-pound payload

- Fly at altitudes of 15,000–25,000 feet

- Provide National Imagery Interpretability Rating Scale (NIIRS) rating of 6 or better at 15,000 feet

- Demonstrate the integration of the SAR system with 1-foot resolution at 15,000 feet.

Initially, the MAE program was described in three phases: the first phase was run by the CIA in order to rapidly prototype a long-endurance UAV based on the Gnat-750, the second phase was led by the UAV JPO for development and management of the original CIA program, and the third phase involved an open competition among UAV contractors for follow-on development and production. During the same time that the MAE program was structured, discussions were conducted on the role of the MAE UAV as a potential advanced technology demonstration—later to be known as an Advanced Concept Technology Demonstration. Although neither the Predator UAV nor the term "ACTD" had been formally associated with the discussions, it was apparent, in hindsight, that this moment could be characterized as the genesis of the role of the Predator as an ACTD.

THE ACTD INITIATIVE

Organization of the Predator program had already started in the fall of 1993, before it had been categorized as an ACTD. However, it became one of the official fiscal year (FY) 1995 ACTD programs when

---

[10]Under Secretary of Defense John M. Deutch, "Endurance Unmanned Aerial Vehicle (UAV) Program," memo to the Assistant Secretary of the Navy for Research, Development and Acquisition, July 12, 1993. Also referred to as the "Deutch Memo."

the ACTD initiative was eventually formalized. In April 1994, a list of the first six candidate ACTDs was published, along with eight other warfighting technologies that were being considered for possible inclusion in the program.[11] As such, the Predator was already structured to satisfy an urgent operational requirement prior to its formalization as an ACTD program.

Because of this timing, the Predator became the de facto prototype of the ACTD process—a process begun in 1994 by the Deputy Under Secretary of Defense for Advanced Technology, in response to recommendations of the Packard Commission in 1986 and the Defense Science Board in 1987, 1990, and 1991. That response took the form of an initiative to provide a process whereby mature technology could be integrated into fieldable prototype systems and provided to operational users for their evaluation of military utility. In a sense, this revolution in military acquisition was due to the belief by acquisition executives that the formal acquisition processes, which are governed by the DoD 5000 Series,[12] were not effective in expediently demonstrating and evaluating new weapon systems. One area cited for specific improvement was the role warfighters played in the development of novel systems.

The Advanced Concept Technology Demonstration not only solicited the inputs of warfighters throughout the entire life of the demonstration, it also included warfighters as part of the management structure of the program and empowered them to determine whether the system met the standards of operational (i.e., military) utility. Although DoD 5000 Series programs had attempted to include user input in the development process, the ACTD process took warfighters' involvement to a new level by providing them with the control over whether or not the program would make the transition to the formal acquisition process. Essentially, the early developer-user interface provided an accelerated means of determining user interest without

---

[11]DUSD/AT, *1995 ACTD Master Plan*, 1995, pp. 1–2.

[12]See especially U.S. Department of Defense, *Defense Acquisition*, DODD 5000.1, March 15, 1996, and *Mandatory Procedures for Major Defense Acquisition Programs (MDAPs) and Major Automated Information System (MAIS) Acquisition Programs*, DoD Regulation 5000.2-R, December 13, 1996.

incurring the cost or time normally spent in a formal acquisition program.

In 1995, a total of 11 ACTDs, including the Predator, were initiated (by Deutch's memo, for the Predator) and funded (by OSD funding, the services, and the defense agencies) for demonstration activities. In 1996, 10 more ACTDs were introduced, with expectations that three other programs would be added later in the year, for a total of 13 (see Table 2.1). Examination of the 1997 ACTD list indicates that 10 efforts have been approved for funding.

The ACTD Niche

Since the ACTD process was initiated in 1994, three components have determined its scope: demonstration of maturing technologies; a focus on warfighters, by allowing heavy user involvement and approval during the entire process; and the execution of the demonstration program itself.

First and foremost, ACTDs are intended to directly rectify weapon-system shortfalls by applying maturing technologies and by including user inputs at all stages of the demonstration process. Unlike formal acquisition programs, ACTDs emphasize the potential for operational capabilities because they are part of actual military deployments. By providing operational users the opportunity to give input into the process and to make their own assessment of the technology, the ACTD process promotes a better understanding of operational utility prior to procurement. Another important outcome of user involvement is that operators are able to develop a corresponding concept of operations as the program matures. After the demonstration program is completed, it is expected that some form of residual asset will exist for operational use.

The second key component of the ACTD process is that warfighter readiness is enhanced by transitioning mature technologies into an operational capability in an efficient manner while satisfying overall affordability goals. Whereas novel technologies in the formal acquisition process pose significant risk to the development community, transition of similar technologies in the ACTD process reduces risk

Table 2.1

ACTDs Approved During FY 1995, FY 1996, and FY 1997

Fiscal Year 1995	Fiscal Year 1996	Fiscal Year 1997
Advanced Joint Planning (AJP)	Air Base/Port Biological Detection	Chemical Enhancement to Bio Detection
Boost Phase Intercept (BPI) (Phase I)	Battlefield Awareness and Data Dissemination (BADD)	Consequence Management
Cruise Missile Defense (Phase I)	Combat Identification	Counterproliferation II
High Altitude Endurance (HAE) UAV	Combat Vehicle Survivability	Extending the Littoral Battlespace
Joint Countermine	Counterproliferation (CP)	Information Warfare Planning Tool
Low Life Cycle Cost Medium Lift Helicopter	Countersniper	Integrated Collection Management
Medium Altitude Endurance UAV (Predator)	Joint Logistics	Joint Helicopter Health and Usage Monitoring System
Precision/Rapid Counter-MRL	Joint Readiness Extension to AJP	Military Operations in Urban Terrain
Precision SIGINT Targeting System	Miniature Air-Launched Decoy Program	Rapid Terrain Visualization
Rapid Force Projection Initiative (RFPI)	Navigation Warfare	Wide Area Tracking System
Synthetic Theater of War (STOW)	Semi-Automated IMINT Processing	
	Tactical High Energy Laser	
	Tactical UAV	

SOURCE: "ACTD Descriptions," http://www.acq.osd.mil/at/descript.htm, September 12, 1997.

because users are intimately involved in the process and can provide immediate feedback.

The third unique aspect of ACTDs is the process by which such programs are planned and executed. Unlike DoD 5000 programs,

ACTDs tend to be short, most lasting from two to four years. In line with the relatively short program timelines, ACTDs require a much more streamlined process to ensure that proper functional areas are planned for during the demonstration. Each ACTD is managed by a service or agency developer and is led by the principal user-sponsor. All warfighter and development organizations are represented in an oversight group of senior representatives chaired by the DUSD/AT. The purpose of this group is to ensure parallel communication among all participants.

Classes of ACTDs

Since the first ACTDs were initiated in 1995, policymakers within the Office of the Secretary of Defense have recognized that all ACTDs do not have identical complexity. Although the primary goal of all ACTDs is to demonstrate mature technology in an operational environment, many different types of systems are chosen as candidates. To better categorize programs and to better understand the types of management and transition issues associated with individual programs, DUSD/AT defined three ACTD classes: software or workstation (Class I), stand-alone system (Class II), and system of systems (Class III).

Class I ACTDs include programs such as the Advanced Joint Planning, the Synthetic Theater of War, and the Battlefield Awareness and Data Dissemination. Expectations for the post-ACTD phase include residual assets produced during the demonstration program. Class II ACTDs are characterized by their focus on a weapon or sensor system and include the Boost Phase Intercept, the High Altitude Endurance UAV, and the Predator UAV (the focus of this study).

If military utility is declared, Class II ACTDs are likely to make a transition into either the Engineering and Manufacturing Development (EMD) or Production phases of the DoD 5000 Series acquisition process. Similar to the Class I ACTD case, Class II programs generally have residual assets after the ACTD process is complete, and these are made available to operational users.

Whereas Class I and Class II programs involve single products, Class III ACTDs generally include multiple weapon systems integrated within an overarching framework. Recent examples of Class III

ACTDs include the Rapid Force Projection Initiative (RFPI) and the Counterproliferation (CP) programs. Besides yielding residual assets after the ACTD program is completed, Class III products are likely to transition to the EMD and Production phases of the 5000 Series acquisition process.

The ACTD Selection Process

As seen in Figure 2.2, the entire ACTD process, including selection and funding, is overseen by the ACTD steering group chaired by the Vice Chief of the Joint Chiefs of Staff (VCJCS) and the Under Secretary of Defense, Acquisition and Technology [USD(A&T)]. Membership in this steering group includes Service Acquisition Executives (SAEs) and Military Operations Deputies. In addition to this oversight, the Joint Warfare Capability Assessment (JWCA) group of the Joint Requirements Oversight Council (JROC) reviews the selection of ACTDs. After selection has been approved, two parallel activities

RAND*MR899-2.2*

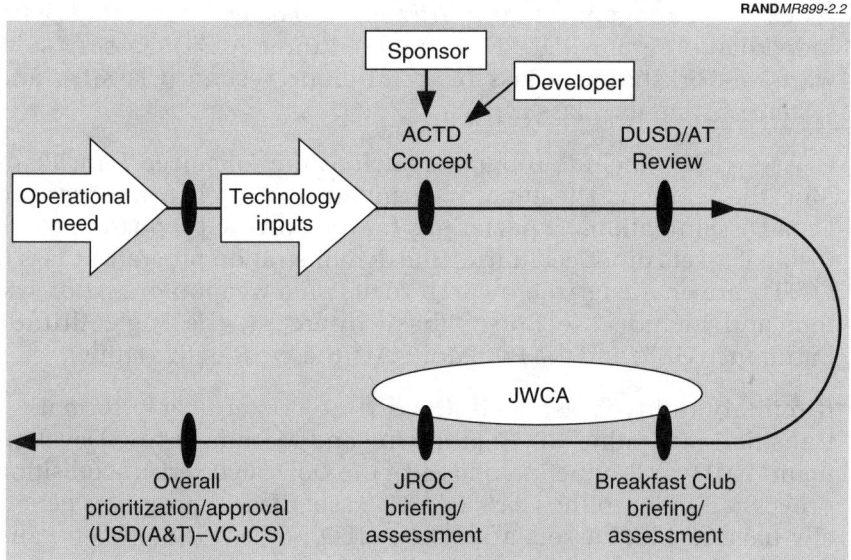

Figure 2.2—The Process for Selecting and Approving ACTDs. Shading indicates the presence of the operational user in all phases.

occur to formalize the ACTD: (1) executive-level approval of program objectives and (2) preparation of the ACTD management plan for the demonstration. This latter requirement serves as the Memorandum of Agreement (MOA) among all parties participating in the ACTD, to ensure that every organization understands its role in the process.

Chapter Three

PROGRAM DESCRIPTION

Whereas Chapter Two provided an overall context for the Predator—history of UAVs, the Tier II lineage, and the ACTD process—this chapter focuses on the facts of the Predator ACTD program to provide a foundation for understanding the types of issues the Predator, as an ACTD, brings to light. In the first section, we describe the origins of the Predator program, give a complete system description, and present major operational events of the ACTD. In the second section, we highlight the business and management aspects of the program, sometimes comparing it informally with acquisition processes. Chapter Four analyzes this information and provides lessons learned that can be applied to other ACTDs for effective management and transition to the formal acquisition process.

ORIGINS AND OVERVIEW OF THE PREDATOR ACTD PROGRAM

Upon receipt of the memorandum signed in July 1993 by Under Secretary of Defense (A&T) John Deutch, which established the initial requirements for the Tier II MAE UAV, the UAV JPO developed program guidelines and established a separate MAE UAV organization. During November 1993, the Deputy Under Secretary of Defense for Advanced Technology directed the JPO to formally solicit bids for the Tier II competition. Expectations for awarding the contract expediently were extremely high. In the memo, the Under Secretary directed the JPO to prepare all documentation so that the contract award for a Tactical Endurance UAV System, meeting all of the Joint Staff's criteria and milestones, could be made within 40 days after money was appropriated.[1] Competitors for the Tier II program included GA-ASI, Teledyne/Ryan/AAI Corporation, TRW/Israel Aircraft Industries, and Lear Astronics Corporation/Scaled Composites, Inc.

Contract Award and Initial Program Schedule

On January 7, 1994, the U.S. Navy by way of the UAV JPO awarded GA-ASI a $31.7-million contract to deliver 10 upgraded Gnat-750 unmanned aerial vehicles for the Tactical Endurance UAV demonstration. During this time as well, the UAV JPO had repeatedly emphasized that the demonstration was just that—an Advanced Concept Technology Demonstration with no immediate expectations to transfer to the acquisition process.

Typical of the guidelines for an ACTD, the program demonstration was expected to be completed within 30 months of the contract award. Likewise, program officials repeatedly referred to the necessity for operational-user inputs into the demonstration process—another hallmark of the ACTD process. As specified in the Predator contract, GA-ASI and the UAV JPO were expected to accomplish the following tasks (Figure 3.1):

- Within 6 months: integrate three aircraft with a ground control station (GCS) and fly them with an electro-optical/infrared (EO/IR) device and ultra-high-frequency (UHF) satellite communications capability.

- Within 18 months: receive four more aircraft and a second GCS. The new aircraft were expected to participate in the fielding either as part of a domestic training exercise such as JTF-95 or in a theater of operations.

- Within 18 months: upgrade one of the first three aircraft to include a synthetic aperture radar in addition to the EO/IR sensor. Replace UHF satellite communications with a Ku-band satellite. Integrate the UAV with the third ground station and fly it.

---

[1]DUSD/AT Larry Lynn, "Tactical Endurance UAV Program," memo to the Assistant Secretary of the Navy for Research, Development & Acquisition, November 17, 1993.

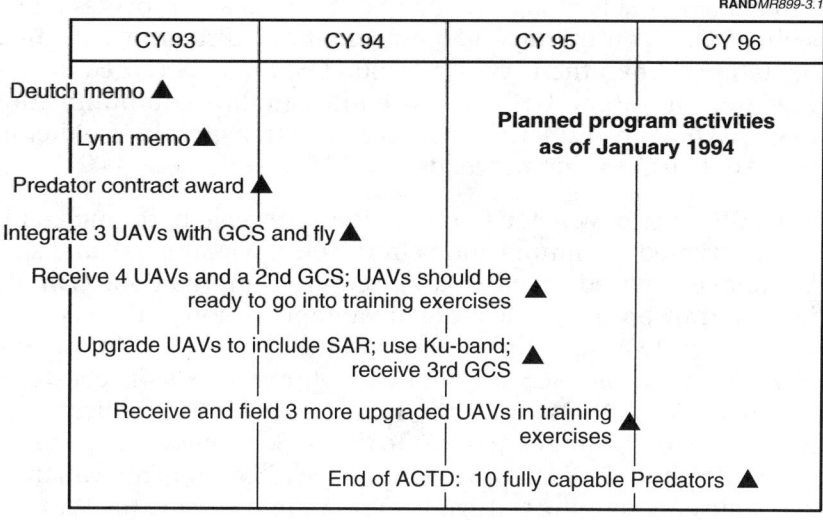

Figure 3.1—Planned Program Event Milestones for Predator

- Within 24 months: receive and field three more upgraded UAVs in training exercises or in-theater. Begin retrofit of the other air-craft.

- Within 30 months: have 10 full-capability tactical endurance UAVs (Predators). According to the original plan, the ACTD was expected to be completed within 30 months. During the ACTD, the JPO was to solicit operational-user input into the program.

The Predator and Its Complementary Systems

Like other UAVs, the Predator UAV relies upon other, complementary systems to ensure effective control and operation during flight. Two main support systems required for the Predator UAV are the ground control station and the Trojan Spirit II (TSII). The GCS is a single trailer containing two pilot/payload-operator consoles and three data-exploitation and mission-planning consoles. While the UAV pilot controls the aerial vehicle during flight, the payload operator monitors sensor readings and captures images. The payload operator also regulates EO/IR functions and camera settings. A

C-band antenna is mounted on top of the GCS and provides line-of-sight (LOS) command and control of the Predator during its operation. When the UAV is beyond LOS, the GCS can control the Predator by either UHF or Ku-band satellite communications (SATCOM). The entire GCS system can be transported in either five C-130 or two C-141 aircraft loads.

The TSII system, which can transmit and receive both unclassified and encrypted communications from voice, wire, digital, and satellite sources, is used primarily to disseminate information. Comprising two transports and two satellite antennas mounted on separate trailers, the TSII functions as a conduit through which information flows between the GCS and the warfighter. The TSII receives air tasking orders (ATOs) from the Joint Force Air Component Commander (JFACC) and relays them to the GCS. Likewise, images taken by the Predator UAV are passed from the GCS to the TSII, which disseminates them to the warfighters for use in assessing the theater of operations. Figure 3.2 shows how the various systems interact within the operational environment.

Major Operational Events of the ACTD

As an ACTD, the major purpose of the Predator program was to demonstrate military utility. Whereas a formal acquisition program would complete initial testing activities in a controlled—i.e., test parameters (weather, flight operations, maneuvers) are strictly defined—and benign environment during its developmental test and evaluation (DT&E) phase, the Predator was tested under operational conditions: in various training exercises and in such conflict sites as Bosnia during Operation Joint Endeavor. This section discusses highlights of the major operational events of the Predator ACTD program.

Following the initial schedule described in Figure 3.1, DoD officials wanted to have a first flight of Predator within 6 months of contract award. Although many considered the task to be daunting, the UAV JPO met the requirement: the Predator flew on July 3, 1994—five days before the 6-month deadline. Its first flight lasted all of 20 seconds. On August 31, 1994, GA-ASI rolled out the Predator for further demonstrations at its El Mirage facility near Victorville, California. From August until October 1994, the Predator logged approximately

RAND*MR899-3.2*

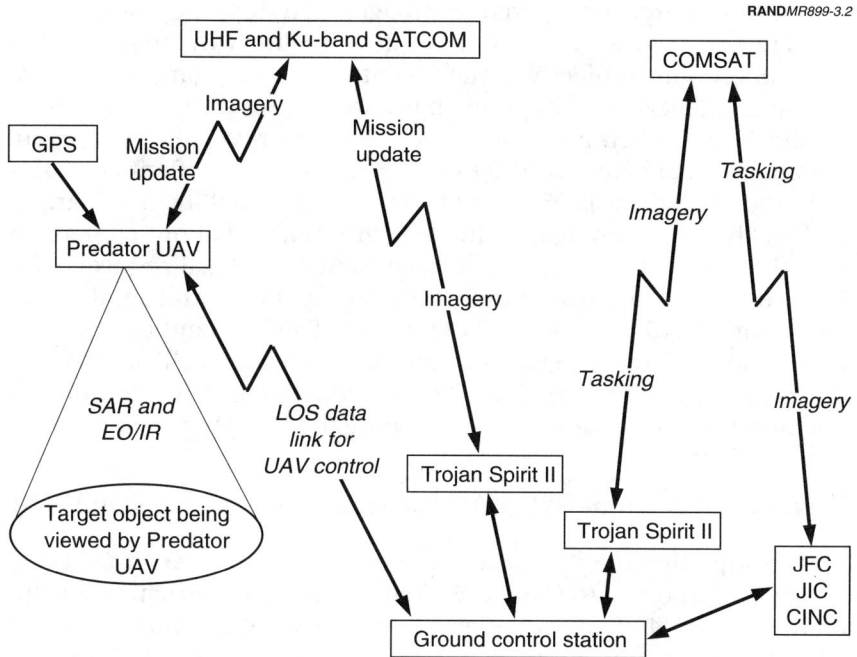

Figure 3.2—The Predator UAV and Its Complementary Systems

85 hours, and, later that fall, flew its first training and operational flight from Fort Huachuca, Arizona, a flight that lasted 40 minutes. In January 1995, the Predator completed a 40-hour, 17-minute flight, setting a new UAV record at the same location.

Roving Sands Exercise

During April and May 1995, the Roving Sands Exercise was held in the southwestern United States, with geographical coverage including Texas and New Mexico. The exercise included aspects of both theater ballistic defense and integrated air defense. The Predator was invited to participate; its specific goal was to try to find simulated Scud-type mobile missiles that were camouflaged against the desert floor.

During the exercise, the Predator logged 170 flight hours and provided reconnaissance on over 200 targets. In line with the goal of fulfilling operational objectives, the Predator surveilled targets and sent real-time imagery to warfighters participating on the ground. Overall, the Predator flew 25 sorties in 26 days and provided 85 percent of the imagery collected for the exercise. According to Pentagon officials, the Predator was 95 percent effective at surveilling fixed targets and picking them up against the background, and about 50 percent effective against mobile, simulated Scuds.[2] The Predator also fulfilled another important milestone during the Roving Sands Exercise: using its45 Ku-band SATCOM link. The Ku band can provide full-motion video of targets through a satellite link to allied forces on the ground. Operational warfighters desired it for surveillance operations like those encountered during the Gulf War.

Predator in Bosnia—NOMAD VIGIL and NOMAD ENDEAVOR

After completing the Roving Sands Exercise in June 1995, the Predator was transported to Gjader Airfield, Albania, to participate in Operation NOMAD VIGIL, at the request of the Secretary of Defense and with approval by the commanders of the United Nations (UN) forces. The introduction of the UAV in Bosnia marked its first participation in a real operational scenario. While in the theater, the Predator was used for reconnaissance and surveillance support for the U.S. European Command (USEUCOM). Although the Predator was initially expected to remain in the theater for 60 days, requests from the operational users caused the system's deployment to be extended to 120 days.

The Predator was considered to be an overwhelming success by the warfighters in Bosnia. However, several areas needing improvement were highlighted during its participation in the operation. As envisioned in the ACTD process, the operational environment was expected to force the developers and users to address issues that would eventually enhance the system. During the Bosnia deployment, a major perception was that the system's sensors were not operating as well as originally anticipated. Problems were attributed to the lack

---

[2]D. A. Fulghum and J. D. Morrocco, "US Readies Predator for Missions in Bosnia," *Aviation Week & Space Technology*, June 5, 1995, p. 22.

of pilot experience, to poor visibility, and to a misunderstanding of how imagery is collected and analyzed.

Another area for improvement that was highlighted by the operational users was the need for the Ku-band capability that had been tested during the Roving Sands Exercise. To fulfill this need and subsequently address the criticism of poor imagery data, the Predator was retrofitted with Ku-band capability in August 1995. After the retrofitting, the UAV could provide real-time motion video to ground sources. According to interviews with warfighters, this addition proved to be of great benefit for surveillance activities. On October 26, 1995, after 120 days in the Bosnia theater, the Predator flew its last mission as part of Operation NOMAD VIGIL and returned to the United States.

After completing a U.S. Customs Service exercise in November 1995 and a Navy exercise called CINCPACFLT COMPTUEX 96-1A in December 1995, the Predator system was again slated to fulfill surveillance missions in Bosnia. Starting its second mission in the region under the control of USEUCOM forces, the Predator supported the Dayton Accords Implementation Force (IFOR) operation known as NOMAD ENDEAVOR. The system was deployed to Taszar, Hungary, and remained there until February 1997.

As indicated in Figure 3.3 and as evidenced by this discussion, the Predator has participated in a myriad of operational scenarios from 1995 through 1996. According to U.S. Atlantic Command sources, such scenarios proved the worthiness of the system by demonstrating its capabilities in the operational environment.

Throughout the ACTD, USACOM, the operational manager, gathered lessons learned from the Predator's operational experience and incorporated them into the actual system, as well as into the system's concept of operations (CONOPS) planning document. The iterative process of learning and incorporating improvements into the system on a real-time basis demonstrated a unique quality of the ACTD process: that operational users had the opportunity to make inputs into the system while assessing its utility.

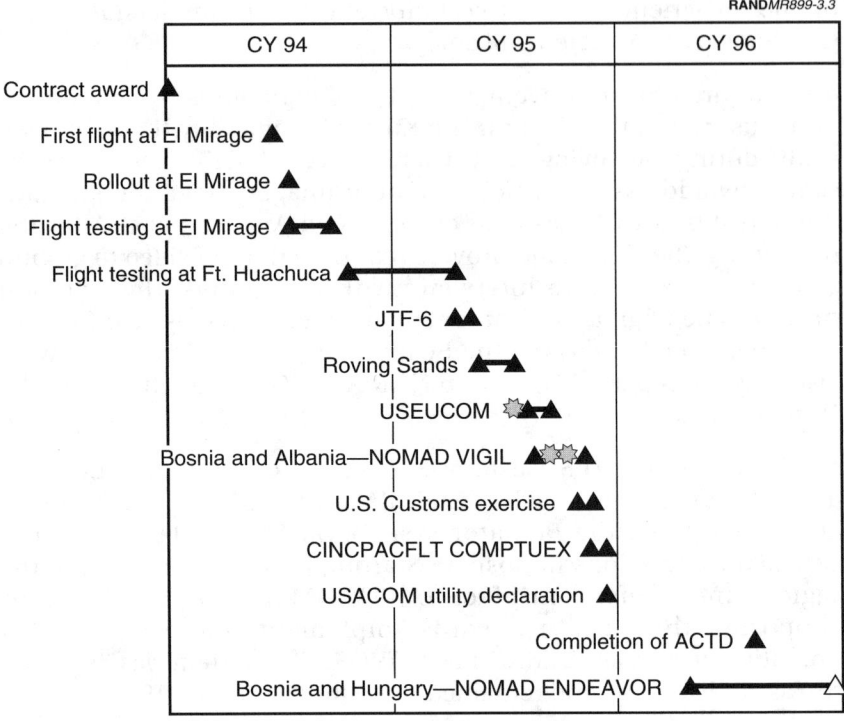

RAND*MR899-3.3*

Figure 3.3—Predator Activities: First Flight to NOMAD ENDEAVOR

BUSINESS AND MANAGEMENT CHARACTERISTICS OF THE PREDATOR ACTD

Just as the system specifications and operational role of the Predator provided information on lessons learned, business and management characteristics of the ACTD point to factors that represent departures from the standard acquisition process and that facilitate the fast pace and other factors contributing to the success of the program. It is the business and management aspects that are, in fact, most important because of their departures from "acquisition as usual." In this section, we describe characteristics that must be considered in any acquisition process: (1) management of the ACTD, (2) communication techniques used by management, (3) operational requirements of the system, (4) testing plans, (5) procurement strategies, (6) funding requirements, and (7) supportability issues.

Management of the Predator ACTD

Several organizations were key to the development and management of the Predator ACTD. Although some of them have already been mentioned, this section briefly summarizes the organizations and reemphasizes the relationships created among them. Government organizations involved in the ACTD include the Deputy Under Secretary of Defense, Advanced Technology (DUSD/AT), the UAV Joint Program Office, U.S. Atlantic Command, U.S. European Command, Air Combat Command, the Defense Advanced Research Projects Agency, the Defense Airborne Reconnaissance Office, the Defense Evaluation Support Activity, and the Air Force Operational Test and Evaluation Center, among others. Government contractors involved in the Predator ACTD include the prime contractor, GA-ASI, and its subcontractors and associate contractors: Boeing, Magnavox, Versatron, Amerind, Westinghouse, and Loral. With responsibility for specific subsystems, each organization played a role in the management and development of the ACTD.

The managing authority for the overarching ACTD process is DUSD/AT, who, in turn, reports to the Under Secretary of Defense, Acquisition and Technology [USD(A&T)]. To effectively manage ACTDs, USD(A&T) developed a policy that required both developers and operational users to be part of the decisionmaking process. In the Predator ACTD, the operational user was represented by a an operational manager, and the development process was headed by a development manager. Per the official ACTD policy, both managers were charged with planning, coordinating, and directing all activities related to the ACTD. The DM focused on the engineering and technical aspects of the program; the OM managed the operational demonstrations and was responsible for assessing the utility of the system. The OM also developed and updated a CONOPS document; established requirements for procurement and production; and carried the title and responsibility of Deputy Demonstration Manager (DDM).

As the developing agency for the Predator ACTD program,[3] the Program Executive Officer for Cruise Missiles and Unmanned Aerial Vehicles within the U.S. Navy was named by the USD(A&T). The PEO(CU) served as the executing agent for acquiring the system and for training personnel at all levels associated with the CONOPS, field operations, and maintenance.[4] Within the PEO(CU), a Navy captain was initially appointed as the DM for the program; later on, a Marine Corps lieutenant colonel filled the position. Unique to the Predator ACTD, the DM served as both the development manager and as Head of the Joint Systems Engineering and Analysis Directorate within the program office. On the operational side of the government management team, USACOM was designated as the operational user of the system. At USACOM, an Army colonel was selected as the OM. As the warfighter representative, USACOM played a major role in setting program priorities among the competing demands of integration, testing, payload development, demonstrations, and real-world deployments. The decision for selecting the DM and the OM was based on USD(A&T)'s assessment of which existing organizations had (1) the right mix of personnel and expertise and (2) were likely to use the Predator system in the future.

In accordance with DoD Directive 5134.11,[5] DARO provided funding and program oversight at the OSD level. Likewise, it was accountable for the development, acquisition, and investment strategies for joint-service and defense-wide airborne reconnaissance activities. Within OSD, an oversight panel was created to monitor the Predator ACTD. The DUSD/AT served as the chairman of the panel, which periodically reviewed program status and ensured that the objectives of the Predator ACTD were being attained efficiently and effectively.

The panel also paid particular attention to the Predator ACTD because of its status as the first such program. It closely monitored the ACTD to ensure that it fulfilled the overarching ACTD vision and that it strictly followed processes established by DUSD/AT and USD(A&T)

---

[3]USD(A&T), "Endurance Unmanned Aerial Vehicle (UAV) Program," memo to ASN (RD&A), July 12, 1993.

[4]USACOM, *USACOM Military Utility Assessment for the MAE UAV ACTD*, Norfolk, Va., May 1996, p. 2.

[5]USD(A&T), *Defense Airborne Reconnaissance Office (DARO)*, Washington, D.C.: DoD Directive 5134.11, April 5, 1995.

policy. Other members of the oversight panel included representatives of the Joint Staff, the services, and DARO. Table 3.1 lists the organizations whose members made up the panel.[6]

Within the UAV JPO, the Predator was managed by the DM, who reported directly to the Deputy PEO for UAVs. Within the Predator ACTD office, five main integrated product teams (IPTs) were responsible for the technical aspects of the ACTD: systems engineering and integration, payloads and data-links engineering, operations and demonstration support, business management, and contracting. The government's IPT structure was mirrored by the contractor, GA-ASI. Coordination between the contractor and the government structures facilitated communication and oversight of the program. Compared with a formal acquisition program, the Predator ACTD was managed by a significantly smaller number of people—10 to 12 as opposed to hundreds. Figure 3.4 shows the organizational relationships on the development side of the Predator ACTD.

Outside of the Predator organization and the operational manager at USACOM, test agencies (DESA and AFOTEC), the Naval Air Systems Command (NAVAIR), and other support organizations participated in the ACTD. To facilitate management agreements between itself and these other organizations, the PEO(CU) developed separate memorandums of agreement, which served as statements of support

Table 3.1

Members of the Oversight Panel for the Predator ACTD

	DUSD(AT) (Panel Chair)
ASN(RD&A)	USEUCOM
DARO	Assistant Secretary of Defense, C3I
Joint Staff (J2)	PEO(CU)/UAV JPO
USACOM/Predator OM	Predator DM
Army/DAMO-FDZ	Air Force/ACC
Army/CECOM	Marines
Navy (N85)	

---

[6]UAV JPO, *Medium Altitude Endurance UAV ACTD Management Plan*, October 1994, p. 8.

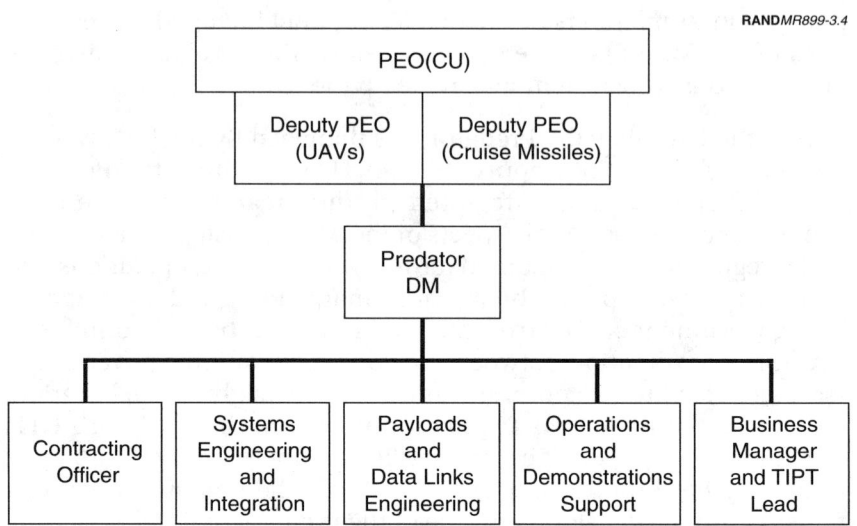

RAND*MR899-3.4*

Figure 3.4—Predator ACTD Organization Chart

for the program from the participating agencies. One example of such an MOA is the Operating Agreement between PEO(CU) and NAVAIR.[7] This document served as a foundation for delineating specific responsibilities for the organizations during the ACTD. From all indications, the use of MOAs, the establishment of an IPT structure, and the small number of personnel involved in the program provided a streamlined management approach that appeared to work well for the Predator ACTD.

Program Management Controls and Communication Techniques

In considering the various mechanisms and approaches used by the government-industry team to manage and control the Predator ACTD, we need to emphasize that an ACTD is not a major acquisition

---

[7]U.S. Navy, Naval Air Systems Command, *Operating Agreement Between the Commander, Naval Air Systems Command and the Naval Aviation Program Executive Officers*, Washington, D.C., August 1990.

program, as are, for example, the F-22, F/A-18E/F, and RAH-66A.[8] Rather, it is more similar to a research and development effort for demonstrating a capability to operational users.

Because of the operational focus of the ACTD process and the aggressively paced milestones of the Predator program, the type and amount of communication could not be expected to be the same as in an acquisition program. Other than an initial government-contractor meeting shortly after contract award in January 1994, the only other formal meetings held between the JPO and GA-ASI were the preliminary design review in February 1994, a critical design review in April 1994, and several flight-readiness reviews before the Predator's first flight in July 1994.

We observed that the Predator DM had a management approach in line with this informal structure, more similar to the type found in research and development initiatives. He emphasized the use of verbal communication between his organization, the OM, and GA-ASI, and relied upon them to provide information expediently if problems arose. Similar to recent emphases in the formal acquisition process to reduce data requirements, very few formal program-documentation requirements were levied on GA-ASI. Some cost/ schedule control system criteria (C/SCSC) reporting was required on the GA-ASI aerial-vehicle contract by the government; however, it was not apparent that the information was used extensively by the DM, the OM, or the contractor team to manage the Predator ACTD. In total, approximately 30 contract data requirements list (CDRL) items were requested. Some of the reduction in CDRL items was attributed to the fact that the Predator system was intended to be an off-the-shelf item with inherently less risk than a new program. Because of the same perception that the Predator was a mature-technology system, no type of formal management plan was used to mitigate risk.

Instead of monitoring the extensive CDRL requests found in formal acquisition programs for program direction, goal-setting, and

---

[8]See Robert V. Johnson and John Birkler, *Three Programs and Ten Criteria: Evaluating and Improving Acquisition Program Management and Oversight Processes Within the Department of Defense,* Santa Monica, Calif.: RAND, MR-758-OSD, 1996, for a more complete description of these formal acquisition programs.

schedule status, the Predator management encouraged informal daily communication. Table 3.2 summarizes the type of control and communication mechanisms used by the management team.

The small size of the government and contractor teams of the Predator ACTD required an *integrated team approach*, which is founded on mutual trust, limited documentation, and novel management techniques. One example of a novel technique is the process by which training was provided to operational users. Instead of the traditional method of using the hardware manufacturer of a system to provide the operational training, subject-matter experts (SMEs) of a second contractor were educated by manufacturing engineers of the prime contractor. This "train the trainers" method took less time out of the schedule for the prime contractor's personnel and likewise provided the subcontractor with enough information to develop an effective training program for aerial vehicle, payload, and maintenance personnel. This initiative allowed the hardware manufacturer to focus on system performance and integration while providing the DM and the OM with a second qualified source of expertise on operational and performance issues of the system.

Table 3.2

Predator Program Control and Communication Techniques

- Medium Altitude Endurance ACTD Management Plan, September 1994

- USACOM CONOPS, June 1996

- Daily communication between government development manager, operational manager, and the GA-ASI program manager (PM)

- Weekly program reviews by phone between the DM and the GA-ASI PM

- Weekly government and contractor staff meetings

- Monthly C/SCSC reporting by GA-ASI to the DM

- Monthly written summary report of technical, schedule, and cost status by the DM to the PEO(CU)

- Quarterly DM program reviews to the PEO(CU)

- Periodic reviews by the OSD Oversight Panel

Documentation of User Requirements by Use of the CONOPS

From its very start, the Predator ACTD focused thoroughly on user requirements rather than on specific system parameters. To rapidly develop, test, and evaluate a system keyed to the operational needs of the Joint Force Commander, USACOM, it combined the efforts of the warfighting and acquisition communities. Initial requirements for the Predator ACTD were expressed in the July 1993 memo from Under Secretary Deutch, and there were few measurable system parameters compared with formal acquisition programs. Likewise, a mature Operational Requirements Document (ORD) was not finished prior to the completion of the ACTD. This is not to imply that there was no need for the system or that warfighters' inputs were not included during the ACTD process. In fact, we observed just the opposite. At the time of its inception, no surveillance system was available that could provide continuous, all-weather coverage of worldwide targets. The Predator filled this gap.

Warfighters' inputs were elicited in CONOPS working groups. In fulfilling its role as the user sponsor, USACOM provided the context and operational scenarios for the demonstration, active-force participants, equipment, and post-demonstration analysis. Throughout the ACTD, USACOM was responsible for writing the Predator CONOPS, which described Predator system characteristics, personnel requirements to operate the UAV, the necessary support infrastructure, intelligence security, scenario options, deployment considerations, and procedures for flight operations. The first CONOPS working group was established in February 1994. It included USACOM, U.S. Southern Command (USSOCOM), the Joint Staff, and UAV JPO personnel. Other services and agencies were invited as well but did not attend. Among participants, the CONOPS facilitated a common understanding of the methods and procedures that the Predator used in the operational environment. Although an initial version was signed by USACOM in May 1994, the CONOPS was considered to be a living document and underwent several iterations in response to Predator's experience in subsequent demonstrations. Examples of system changes that were incorporated into the revised CONOPS include such ice-mitigating mechanisms on the aerial vehicle as ice sensors, a modified engine inlet, and heated pitot tubes.

However, a CONOPS by all accounts is not an ORD. Whereas a CONOPS may be appropriate during the ACTD, it is inadequate for carrying the program through the acquisition process. The ORD is intended to provide both the user and the development manager with a future reference by which the system's performance can be judged. For example, an ORD would describe the need for a UAV to fly at certain altitudes with a specific type of sensor payload to accomplish a unique mission over a certain geographical territory. According to traditional acquisition practices, an ORD is required for a program to exist. During our interviews with program personnel, many questioned the need for an ORD in the ACTD process, given that the system had already been developed, flown, and fielded. Many organizations felt that if they were required to develop an ORD, the document would be nothing more than a back-filling exercise of the technical configuration of the Predator. We tend to disagree with this assessment, and elaborate on this point in Chapter Four.

Choosing a Lead Service

After the ACTD is complete, the lead service essentially "takes the reins" from the user-sponsor, USACOM, assuming operational responsibility for the system by providing personnel, training, and support equipment. Per USD(A&T) policy, it was necessary for a lead service to be chosen prior to transition of the ACTD into the formal acquisition process. Although the policy stated the need for declaring a lead service prior to transition, there was no OSD guidance for selecting the lead service, a time frame for when the lead should be declared, or how much the service should be involved with the program prior to its designation as the lead. As the Predator ACTD continued and the CONOPS was being developed in 1994–1995, USACOM expressed concern that potential lead services had not been intimately involved with either the Predator ACTD or the development of the Predator CONOPS.

In December 1995, the Vice Chairman of the Joint Chiefs of Staff wrote a JROC Memorandum to the Secretary of Defense, indicating that the Air Force and its Air Combat Command had been chosen as the lead service for the Predator UAV.[9] Aside from the Air Force, other competitors included the Forces Command (FORSCOM) of the Army and the Commander in Chief of the Atlantic Fleet (CINCLANTFLT) of the Navy.

Many of the people we interviewed thought that the timing of this decision was late. Most of their consternation was because the USAF had not actively participated in the development of the CONOPS or the operational demonstration in Bosnia. As a result, the Air Force by way of its representative, ACC, did not have the institutional knowledge to lead the program after the ACTD was completed. Similarly, the Air Force had not provided recommendations for system enhancements prior to its designation as the lead service.

On this last point, the ACC indicated three operational requirements that were not incorporated as part of the ACTD: (1) a de-icing system based on USAF standards, (2) a two-way VHF/UHF air control radio, and (3) an Identification Friend or Foe (IFF) Mode IV capability suitable for USAF operations. It is not clear why USACOM, as the user-sponsor, had not incorporated these requests into the ACTD, except that it may not have fully understood the unique needs of the Air Force. Many felt that if ACC had either taken a more proactive role or if the USAF had been designated as the lead service earlier, general requirements such as these—requirements that ACC perceived to be part of the overall definition of the military utility of the system—would not have been overlooked.

In lieu of the CONOPS, ACC began to develop an ORD that specified Air Force needs such as those mentioned above. However, the current draft of the ORD requires a Predator system that is more robust (i.e., focuses more on logistics, has more specifications, contains 100 more pages of ORD material) than what was demonstrated during the ACTD.

---

[9]William A. Owens, Admiral, Vice Chairman of the Joint Chiefs of Staff, JROCM 151-95, memo to the Honorable William J. Perry, December 16, 1995, paragraph 1.

Determination of Military Utility

As the preceding discussion attests, the task of defining what constitutes *military utility* is daunting to say the least. No formal policy exists for determining how utility should be declared. Similarly, there is no guidance on whether or not utility should be declared before or after the lead service has been selected. Both of these policy gaps presented problems for the Predator ACTD. The only reference by USD(A&T) to utility declaration is that "the user-sponsor is responsible for assessing the worth of an ACTD."[10]

This issue carries even greater weight in the Predator case, because the ACC disagreed with the Predator CONOPS and the system specification after the USAF was designated as the lead service. To define a utility-specification process, USACOM took the lead as the operational user and, working with other participants, developed a matrix for assessing the Predator's accomplishments. As seen in Figure 3.5, the matrix included those ACTD objectives expressed in the CONOPS and contrasted them against those major activities in which the Predator participated. After assessing the fulfillment of the ACTD objectives subjectively (i.e., with no quantitative methodology), USACOM declared that the Predator had demonstrated military utility in every event in which it had participated.

Testing of the Predator

Compared with formal acquisition programs, developmental testing (DT) and operational test and evaluation (OT&E) are not required for ACTDs. In fact, if all the usual activities that constitute the formal acquisition process were compared and contrasted with the ACTD process, the testing activity could be characterized as one of the more creative and unbounded areas, primarily because the goal of the ACTD process is different from that of the formal acquisition process. Whereas the former attempts to determine military utility, the latter hopes to field a system that is in compliance with rigid testing criteria and standards. Testing in the ACTD environment is focused on what the user wants to see done. In the Predator ACTD,

---

[10]USD(A&T), *Advanced Concept Technology Demonstrations Master Plan,* Washington, D.C., August 1996, p. 1-5.

RANDMR899-3.5

CONOPS Objective	Activity								
	JTF-6 (8 Feb–19 Mar 95)	RS 95 (29 Apr–8 May 95)	USSOCOM (12–22 Jun 95)	EUCOM (6 Jul–29 Oct 95)	Customs (20 Oct–4 Nov 95)	Tomahawk OTL (Various)	COMPTUEX (20 Nov–10 Dec 95)	EUCOM (Mar–Dec 96)	USN/SSN (June 96)
Special Operations Support		×	×						
Amphibious/Expeditionary Support							×		
Forward Air Control Operations/ Close Air Support									
Air Patrol									
Theater Missile Defense									
Major Ground Battle		×							
Counterdrug Support	×	×			×				
Targeting Support Battle Damage Assessment		×		×		×			
Air Defense				×					
War at Sea							×		×
Combat Search and Rescue				×			×		
Direct Support to Military Intelligence Brigade		×		×					
Medium–High Tempo Operations		×		×					
Real-World Support				×				×	×
DoD Support to Other Federal Agencies	×				×				
Direct Broadcast Technology Evaluation		×					×	×	×

SOURCE: USACOM, *USACOM Military Utility Assessment for the MAE UAV ACTD*, Norfolk, VA., May 1996, p. 17.

NOTE: × signifies that objective was attained.

Figure 3.5—CONOPS Objective/Exercise-Activity Matrix

this testing was accomplished primarily in an operational environment.

Two government test organizations, DESA and AFOTEC, were heavily involved during the demonstration of the Predator. DESA was chartered in July 1990 by the Deputy Under Secretary of Defense to provide planning, test support, and evaluation capabilities to DoD and non-DoD government activities. Unlike other government test organizations, DESA characterizes itself as a "qualitative tester," because it assesses utility as opposed to determining if specific requirements are met. DESA began its involvement in the Predator program in fall 1994 and finished its testing role at the end of the ACTD in July 1996. The Predator UAV represents the first ACTD in which DESA participated.

AFOTEC, the other major test organization involved with the Predator ACTD, is a unit that reports directly to the Air Force Chief of Staff. As the Air Force's independent test agency, it is responsible for the operational testing of new systems being developed for the Air Force as well as by multi-service users. AFOTEC began its participation in the Predator program after being directed by the Secretary of Defense. It was expected to accomplish the following:

- Impart operational test experiences to ACTDs.

- Assist in developing measures of effectiveness/performance (MOEs/MOPs).

- Assess and preserve demonstration data for use as a baseline for the formal acquisition process.

- Make recommendations for system improvement.

- Identify strengths and weaknesses in the areas of system effectiveness and suitability.

- Assess the readiness of the ACTD system for transition to the formal acquisition process.

- Assist in developing an ORD and a CONOPS for the Predator.[11]

---

[11]AFOTEC, *Policy for Advanced Concept Technology Demonstrations,* Kirtland AFB, N.M.: HQ AFOTEC/CC, Policy Letter 96-02, April 5, 1996.

Likewise, DUSD/AT requested that AFOTEC conduct an operational assessment (OA) of the Predator ACTD (described in the following subsection). The purpose of the OA was to identify areas of risk, characterize the system, assess the potential for operational effectiveness and suitability, and determine readiness for possible production and OT&E.[12] Eight months prior to AFOTEC's involvement with the Predator, DESA had also conducted an OA for DUSD/AT during the UAV's first deployment to Bosnia. Together, both the DESA and the AFOTEC OAs were intended to furnish additional information for determining the military utility of the Predator. A secondary purpose of the OAs was to provide a foundation for testing in the formal acquisition process.

During discussions with program personnel, the late timing of AFOTEC involvement in the ACTD assessment process arose as an issue similar to that arising from ACC's late entrance into the Predator ACTD. Many felt that AFOTEC also should have participated earlier in the testing of the system. To the credit of both test organizations, any problems that may have been created by the delayed entry were well masked by the close-knit working relationship between DESA and AFOTEC. Specifically, they had MOAs that facilitated the sharing of information and experiences in order to expedite the OA process. The close coordination between the two appeared to be key to AFOTEC's finishing its operational assessments even though it had been brought into the program late. Figure 3.6 shows the key operational-assessment dates and locations in which both AFOTEC and DESA participated.

Purpose of the Predator OA: Scope and Relationship to Formal Testing

During the Predator demonstrations, formal test-planning documents, such as test and evaluation master plans (TEMPs) and test matrices, were not developed. Likewise, very few rules were set for the government and contractor to follow during the two operational assessments, which implied that an organization such as USACOM was fully in charge of the assessment process. The government and

---

[12]AFOTEC, *AFOTEC MAE UAV Operational Assessment Report*, Kirtland AFB, N.M., June 24, 1996, p. 3.

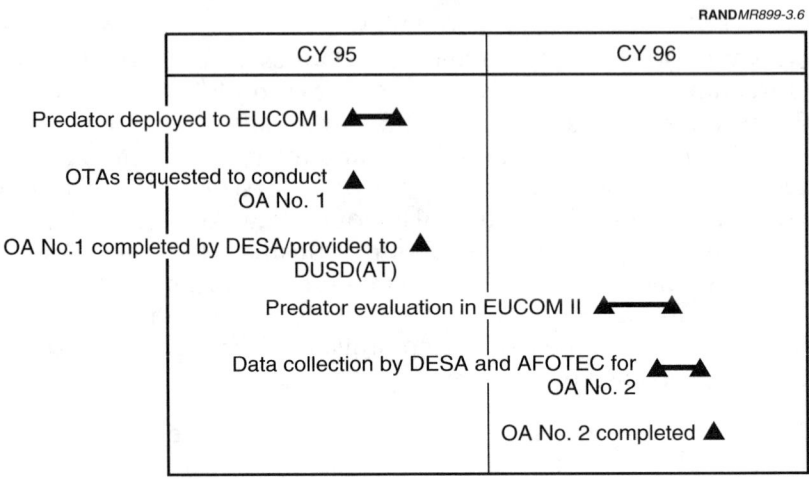

Figure 3.6—Major Milestones for Operational-Assessment Activities

the contractor made final decisions on the types and number of sorties that the Predator would fly; DESA and AFOTEC served as references for test information and support.

An OA also differs from a formal test in another important aspect: the amount of contractor and government involvement during testing activities. Whereas personnel from the system contractor's facility are not allowed to participate in testing activities in a formal acquisition program, the ACTD allowed for contractor, UAV JPO, DESA, and AFOTEC involvement. For example, the government and GA-ASI gave supplementary assistance in the form of spare parts, maintenance of the system, and technical guidance to ensure that the Predator was ready and capable of flight. Such involvement is awkward, given that the contractor is not going to be present in battle, and it poses an interesting issue for transition: How much of the data collected during the OA can be used during testing in the formal acquisition process, given that the system was significantly aided during the demonstration?

Derivation of Effectiveness Parameters for the Predator ACTD

The measures developed by the government test organizations and used in their operational assessment of the Predator ACTD could be viewed as operational requirements, because, since the UAV did not have an ORD, the Predator program had no formal specifications. In lieu of assessing requirements, DESA and AFOTEC developed surrogate measures. The evaluation criteria were created through a review of "reference inputs"—the Predator CONOPS, the 1993 Predator Mission Needs Statement (MNS), the DARO UAV Program Plan, the DARO Integrated Airborne Reconnaissance Strategy (IARS)—and the experience of DESA and AFOTEC personnel.

Organized like a work breakdown structure (WBS), measures were defined to the lowest level of evaluation criteria. As indicated by AFOTEC, the purpose of these measures was to assess the military utility of the Predator; they were not intended for defining future program requirements during the formal acquisition process. However, examination of the measures of success revealed that qualitative questions and statements were used for the most part in constructing them. Similar to the issue raised under the section on military utility, no policy guidance existed for developing accurate evaluation criteria. Figure 3.7 shows the relationship between the hierarchy of measures and the reference inputs used by DESA and AFOTEC.

Procurement Strategy

Assumed in the procurement strategy for the Predator was that the system was a commercial off-the-shelf item. Responding to the aggressive ACTD schedule that required a contract decision within 40 days of funding availability,[13] the OSD awarded a cost-plus-fixed-fee contract for the aerial vehicle to GA-ASI in January 1994. Sepa-

---

[13]DUSD/AT, "Tactical Endurance Unmanned Aerial Vehicle (UAV) Program," memo to the ASN(RD&A), November 17, 1993.

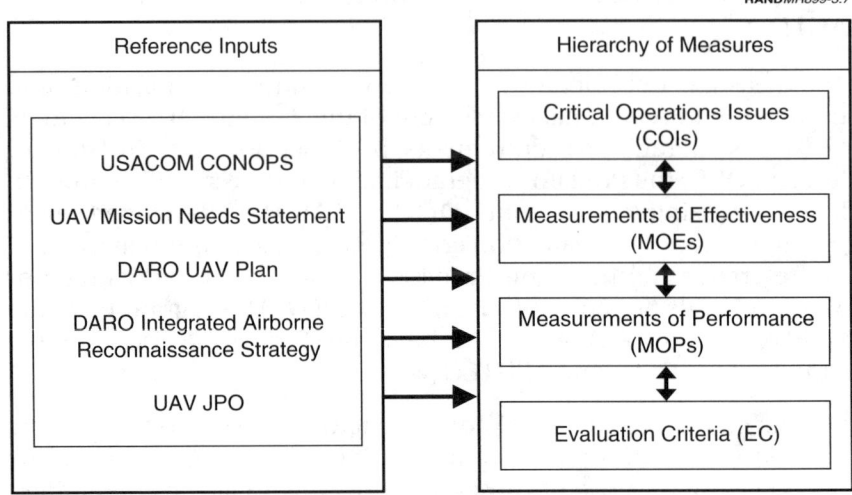

RAND*MR899-3.7*

Figure 3.7—Operational-Assessment Measures Used for the Predator ACTD

rate contracts were awarded for the SAR, wideband common data link, and other mission support equipment. As specified in the contracts, the JPO assumed the entire integration risk for the Predator system—something that is rarely done in formal acquisition programs.

Since the primary goal of the Predator ACTD was, from the outset, to demonstrate military utility, the JPO and other oversight organizations gave minimal consideration to post-ACTD efforts. Instead, the JPO planned only for support of the residual assets of the ACTD: 10 aerial vehicles, three ground control stations, and three Trojan Spirit IIs. Consequently, no options for additional hardware were written into the initial contracts with GA-ASI or its subcontractors.

Likewise, producibility initiatives and design-to-cost issues that are usually addressed in formal acquisition programs were ignored. The procurement strategy was more closely related to those associated with research and development efforts, emphasizing achievement of technical goals within a strict schedule.

Affordability Considerations

As with the procurement strategy, a long-term view was also missing in affordability considerations. The demonstration manager and other government officials paid little attention to issues of affordability during the Predator ACTD, to which acquisition policies on cost-performance trade-offs[14] and life-cycle cost[15] did not apply because it was not a formal acquisition program. Consequently, cost as an independent variable (CAIV) was never considered as a criterion.

Funding *was* a consideration, however. Funding increments are based on JPO estimates. When the Predator ACTD was first begun, it received an initial funding increment through DUSD/AT based on JPO estimates. After FY 94, the resource sponsor responsible for funding the Predator was the Defense Airborne Reconnaissance Office.[16] Unlike formal acquisition programs, the UAV JPO received its funding directly from DARO and not through the component Planning, Programming, and Budgeting System (PPBS). The ACTD benefited from this distinction because it received its funding directly from the DoD, as opposed to risking the loss of monies if controlled by and funneled through the individual services.

As an ACTD, the Predator was a 30-month program whose residual assets were expected to be used for further testing, training, and deployment. No detailed planning for transitioning the Predator was begun until a transition integrated product team (TIPT) was formed in the summer of 1995. Given that the system was considered COTS and that there was little pressure to control program costs, cost issues appear to have been a lesser concern than achieving schedule and meeting technical performance criteria.

The only cost figure the JPO considered during the ACTD was associated with the aerial vehicle. The JPO estimated the flyaway target cost for the Predator in the $3–$3.5-million range. However, in April 1996, the Predator TIPT reported that the cost of a Predator system, including four aerial vehicles, a ground control station, one Trojan

---

[14]USD(A&T), "Policy on Cost-Performance Trade-Offs," memo, July 19, 1995.

[15]USD(A&T), "Reducing Life Cycle Costs for New and Fielded Systems," memo, December 4, 1995.

[16] See USD(A&T), DoD Directive 5134.11, April 5, 1995, for a full description.

Spirit II system, operator training, and logistics support, was around $30 million.[17] Prior to the release of this information, the Air Force, as the lead service for the Predator, did not realize that significant life-cycle costs would be associated with the entire system. Needless to say, a great deal of consternation grew out of the cost estimate. Because detailed LCC estimates—a normal part of program oversight in the formal acquisition process—had never been prepared by the program or the contractor, the management team was caught short in providing higher-level officials with accurate estimates of why the Predator program costs were higher than those previously reported by the JPO.

Besides the absence of a detailed LCC estimate, other definitional mistakes (e.g., giving the wrong type of estimate) were made by JPO when cost figures were being released. On several occasions, the JPO was unable to adequately explain why specific systems cost as much as they did. In essence, it could not track costs to specific components although it was receiving C/SCSC information from GA-ASI. This inconsistency hampered proper resource planning. As a consequence, it appeared that the Predator ACTD would not have adequate funding for support activities for the originally planned number of residual systems. In the short run, the solution to the funding shortage was to procure fewer Predator systems than were originally planned for.

Funding Requirements

The estimated baseline Predator ACTD cost was $112 million. This cost did not include replacement aircraft or logistics support for future years, costs that—when added to the baseline estimate—bring the total program cost through FY 99 to $147 million. However, the FY 95 program objective memorandum (POM) funding profile, shown in Table 3.3, did not include any programmed funding for follow-on Predator activities. USD(A&T) recognized this shortcoming and is in the process of addressing the transition-phase funding requirement alternatives to ensure that appropriate funding exists.

---

[17] *Inside the Pentagon*, April 25, 1996, p. 8.

Table 3.3

Predator POM 95 ($ millions)

	94	95	96	97	98	99	Total
Predator UAV	40	39	13	0	0	0	92
Operational Exercises	0	3	4	0	0	0	7
Demonstrations	0	0	3	10	0	0	13
Replacement A/C & Support	0	0	0	10	15	10	35
	40	42	20	20	15	10	147
	PEO(CU) PE		DARO PE				

For the most part, funding was stable because of the high level of support from the Joint Chiefs of Staff (JCS), the operational user, and the OSD for the Predator ACTD. Unlike with many other ACTDs and formal acquisition programs, major funding perturbations did not occur.[18] Consequently, the Predator ACTD proceeded as initially planned. In program execution, however, there was a 6-percent cost overrun—a small amount when compared with similarly sized, yet riskier, research and development programs.

Supportability of the Predator

Formal acquisition programs are required to determine supportability plans, conduct logistics support analysis (LSA) tasks, and perform life-cycle cost estimates; ACTD programs are not. This was evident in the Predator ACTD as well. The fast pace and relatively short schedule of the ACTD process made it difficult to adequately determine long-term logistics requirements. Similarly, the primary focus of the ACTD was on the demonstration of technology—and the technical performance of the system—and not on how supportable or maintainable the system was. The determination of Predator's military utility by USACOM had virtually nothing to do with logistics or LCC issues.

---

[18]See Johnson and Birkler, 1996, for a discussion of funding perturbations and their effect on such programs as the Air Force F-22, Navy F/A-18, and Army RAH-66.

The supportability and logistics planning that did occur in the Predator ACTD was facilitated by CONOPS review meetings. USACOM and the UAV JPO invited operational users for discussions on the operation of the Predator. Inputs were given by the participants, coordinated, and later included into the CONOPS. However, our review of the CONOPS indicated that the only supportability issue that was adequately documented was deployment of the Predator system. Discussions of training, maintainability, human factors, and reliability of the system were minimal. It appeared that the JPO and USACOM were content with postponing addressing these issues until the USAF took over as the operator of the system. Unfortunately, as previously noted, the USAF had not participated extensively in the CONOPS meetings, nor, for that matter, had it been involved in discussions of how to plan for the supportability of the Predator.

Discussions with government personnel also highlighted the fact that there was minimal information regarding the failure rates of the Predator, its material composition, handling instructions for shipping and transportation, and other maintenance techniques. Although the pilots were provided flight operations manuals (not formal Dash-1s, which tell pilots how to start the plane, deal with emergencies in flight, and shut down the plane) prepared by GA-ASI, no repair manuals or technical orders were created for maintenance personnel. Similarly, the government did not know the reliability of the Predator in terms of failure rates at either the line-replaceable-unit (LRU) or shop-replaceable-unit (SRU) level. No documents were prepared to show the types of spare parts required for the Predator.

As with other ACTD programs, the iterative nature of the Predator ACTD was intended to incorporate operational perspectives into the design. However, it was not clear that human-factors issues, especially supportability issues, were included as the Predator design evolved. Documentation provided by DESA[19] and AFOTEC[20] showed

---

[19]DESA, *Medium Altitude Endurance (MAE) Unmanned Aerial Vehicle (UAV) Advanced Concept Technology Demonstration (ACTD) Recommendations History,* Washington, D.C., August 2, 1996.

[20]AFOTEC, *MAE UAV (Predator) Operational Assessment Updated Report,* Kirtland AFB, N.M., June 24, 1996.

that recommendations had been made, but most focused on the operator's requests, not the maintainer's. Some examples are relocating the GCS main entrance door to the rear to block out light, redesigning the pilot and payload-operator stations to ergonomic standards, improving the software to facilitate operator interface with the terminal, and modifying the pilot-operator station so that it resembled a modern aircraft cockpit.

To ensure support of the Predator system during operational scenarios, the JPO set up a contractual relationship via a maintenance agreement with GA-ASI to provide contractor logistics support (CLS) during the entire ACTD. Although the original intent of this agreement was for the contractor to supplement military maintenance technicians during deployments, the contractor played the primary maintenance role. GA-ASI trained military personnel to use and fix the Predator system, because the government did not have reliability or engineering data for the UAV. This lack raised the question, What will happen when the program makes the transition to the formal acquisition process? Other questions follow: Will logistics and supportability requirements be reconsidered? If so, will such requirements force a redesign of the system? How much will such redesign cost? Should more time be spent up front in the ACTD to address some of the more pressing logistics concerns or wait until the transition or formal acquisition phases to do so? Answers to these questions are addressed in Chapter Four.

Manpower and Personnel Training

Not only must the kind of support needed be addressed, but the quantity: How many and what type of skilled personnel would be needed to operate the Predator system? In the CONOPS, the JPO and USACOM specified that each Predator detachment would require a total of 38 people: 10 officers and 28 noncommissioned officers. Of the 38, 6 were operators and mission planners, 6 were maintenance technicians, 12 were sensor and imagery analysts, 9 operated the TSII, and 5 provided miscellaneous support.

However, the number 38 did not include the contractor personnel required to support the system during the operational demonstrations. Given that GA-ASI, DESA, and AFOTEC had assisted with the operation of Predator during its demonstrations, it is not clear whether 38 people would actually be enough to run the Predator autonomously. In order to augment the initial personnel requirements, USACOM sent out various messages in March 1995 to all of the services, indicating that 114 personnel were required to run three detachments. Guidance from USACOM also described specific occupational billets needed for the detachments. Via the JPO, the services assigned personnel to the Predator detachments on a temporary basis: All operators and maintainers of the Predator were on TDY status.

As to training, no plans had been formulated at the beginning of the ACTD that could effectively handle the throughput of the number of people required for deployment. However, the JPO and USACOM had, by the end of the ACTD in July 1996, defined, established, and conducted various pilot-training sessions at Ft. Huachuca, Arizona. The subcontractor subject-matter experts created and taught all training, which was developed in accordance with MIL-STD-1379D.[21]   Specific sections of the training were tailored to accommodate the Predator. All course material was reviewed by the UAV Joint Training Center at Ft. Huachuca. The first training class commenced in October 1994 and lasted until March 1995. A second course was taught June–August 1995, and a third session was held in November 1995. The JPO and USACOM had apparently developed thorough game plans for pilot training. The only limits to the training throughput were system availability, GA-ASI support capacity, and SME availability.

Although training appeared to be operating smoothly from a throughput perspective, other aspects of the training posed difficulties. First, the services had different opinions of who could fly the Predator, because the JPO and USACOM did not establish any uniform standards for its operation. The Navy and Army nominated only rated pilots for the position. The Air Force, however, was allowing navigators as well as pilots to apply because it could not find enough pilots. Second, military pilots were never fully certified by training representatives from GA-ASI for solo flights. The government pilots never achieved what GA-ASI believed to be an adequate number of sorties for full certification: 50 landings of the Predator.

---

[21]UAV JPO, "Predator: MAE IPT Briefing," June 26, 1995.

Consequently, if military pilots were flying the UAV, the government incurred whatever liability was caused by problems with the system. From the government perspective, it appeared that GA-ASI had mitigated its risks for any major system liability by instituting this 50-landing clause in the contract.

SIMILAR DETAILS, DIFFERENT PROCESSES

As a military acquisition program, the Predator UAV had many characteristics that are typical of a more formalized research and development program. In fact, at first glance, the untrained eye may not recognize that the program was not governed by the same type or number of rules that formal acquisition programs are required to follow. However, further inspection into the workings of the organization reveals a management system and program structure that are relatively more flexible and less constrained than what would be encountered in a formal analog, including minimal CDRLs, a small program office, and less-frequent formal reviews with the contractor. Although there were generally not as many rules to follow, the success of the Predator UAV ACTD was based on the ability of program managers to effectively and efficiently execute functional aspects, including technical integration, fiscal budgeting, and operational assessments—activities that must be completed in a formal acquisition program as well.

Essentially, an underlying message that applies to all acquisition programs could be drawn from this observation, regardless of whether or not the programs are pre-acquisition or of a more formal type: Certain activities must be accomplished to ensure success. The next chapter highlights some of the activities and areas that we perceived to be important to the success or detriment of the Predator UAV ACTD and that should also be considered for other ACTDs.

Chapter Four

ISSUES FRAMEWORK

The preceding chapters have highlighted a variety of issues that arose at various stages of the Predator ACTD, in various areas, and with various participants. In this chapter, we (1) highlight portions of the program that could be generalized and used as lessons learned for the benefit of other ACTDs and (2) detail and tabulate the similarities and differences between the Predator ACTD and a typical formal acquisition program.

The preceding chapters reveal two general types of issues arising from the ACTD: demonstration issues and transition issues. The first type is associated with the management of the Predator during its ACTD phase and encompasses aspects of the program that could facilitate an effective demonstration. The second type of issue is associated with the Predator ACTD as it proceeds to the formal acquisition process. Together, these two general types of issues provide a robust set of lessons that can be applied to other ACTDs to aid both the successful demonstration of ACTDs and their transition to the formal acquisition process.

ACTD DEMONSTRATION ISSUES

Demonstration issues relate to those events, situations, or decisions that either enhanced or detracted from the successful demonstration of the Predator during its ACTD phase. Table 4.1 provides a summary of the subjects and associated issues that are discussed in this section, in the order presented in the text.

Table 4.1

Demonstration Issues

Subject	Issues
Choice of demonstration and operational managers	• Skills base • Mutual relationship
Characteristics of the government program office	• Size of organization • Use of MOAs to create a virtual organization • Selection of personnel with experience
Measures of program control	• Emphasis on informal communication • CDRL items
Selection of lead service	• Timing of decision • Methodology of choice
Declaration of military utility	• Timing in relation to selection of lead service • Qualitative or quantitative methodology
Stability of funding	• Funding considerations throughout ACTD
Personnel requirements	• Service commitment • Uniformity of skills • Training
Involvement of Operational Test Agencies (OTAs)	• Timing of involvement • Benefits of operational testing

Choice of Demonstration and Operational Managers

The demonstration manager (DM) and the operational manager (OM) served as the co-managers of the Predator ACTD. Although different in scope and responsibility, both positions were critical to the success of the ACTD. Similarly, the use of the OM in the decision process added an operational focus to the ACTD that is not usually demonstrated in formal acquisition programs.

We found two important issues associated with the selection of the DM and the OM in the Predator ACTD: (1) care should be taken to select individuals with the right skills and background for the job and (2) as with other programs, a good working relationship between the two managers facilitated success.

Issue: Skills Base. Because ACTDs are pre-acquisition efforts and are not required to follow Defense Acquisition Workforce Improvement Act (DAWIA) requirements, formally defined rules for selecting program managers do not apply. As a result, individuals without the right type of background could be selected to lead an ACTD.

Recommendation: As a demonstration effort, the ACTD is focused on technology. And because the ACTD does not follow the rules of formal acquisition, the DM must have a background in and understanding of program management and the DoD 5000 Series, as indicated in Table 4.2. At the very least, an engineering background supplemented by previous program office experience and the Defense Systems Management Course (DSMC) would be beneficial.

Issue: Mutual Relationship. The DM and the OM for the Predator were competent, confident, effective, innovative, and efficient at accomplishing their tasks. Similarly, each individual had a background that fulfilled the criteria listed above. At USACOM, the OM worked well with the warfighter community in fostering user inputs into the ACTD. At the JPO, the DM was well-versed in acquisition fundamentals, yet had the ability to work within the flexibility of the ACTD process to ensure a successful demonstration.

Recommendation: Although difficult to foresee, we recommend that DMs and OMs also be chosen according to their ability to work with one another in achieving the goals of the demonstration. The Predator DM and OM had a very close working relationship, which aided in resolving problems and facilitated the process for addressing program and operational issues. Similarly, in an interservice context, the joint leadership of the duo bypassed the potential for secrets and undesirable turf battles.

This issue is important for all classes of ACTDs and is readily apparent in the Predator. However, it becomes even more important for Class III ACTDs, for which coordination, multiple managers,

Table 4.2

Attributes Desired of an ACTD Demonstration Manager

Criteria	Requirement
Technical knowledge closely related to the ACTD	Desirable
Program management experience	Mandatory
Test and evaluation experience	Desirable
Test and evaluation knowledge	Mandatory
Research and development experience	Desirable
Research and development knowledge	Mandatory
Excellent communication skills	Mandatory
Experience with integrating multiple systems	Mandatory
Operational background	Desirable

SOURCE: Robert V. Johnson and Michael R. Thirtle, "Management of Class III Advanced Concept Technology Demonstration (ACTD) Programs: An Early and Preliminary View," unpublished RAND research.

different PEOs, and a myriad of systems require an integrated management approach.

Characteristics of the Government Program Office

Relative to formal acquisition programs, we observed three unique aspects of the Predator program office within the UAV JPO: (1) to function, the ACTD did not require a large government program office to manage the program, (2) MOAs were used to increase the virtual size of the organization, and (3) individuals with appropriate expertise were selected to run the program.

Issue: Size of Organization. Within the government, 10–12 people were assigned directly to the Predator ACTD full-time. Although a small number relative to formal acquisition programs, this did not deter the organization from successfully managing the program. On the contrary, the small number of people were effective in carrying out their responsibilities.

Issue: MOAs to Create Virtual Organization. To augment the Predator staff, the DM and the OM also utilized MOAs to deflect responsibility for certain functions to other agencies. For example, most of the test planning was done by DESA and AFOTEC, which enabled the Predator organization to staff fewer test personnel than it would have been required to do otherwise. MOAs assisted during events such as the Preliminary Design Review (PDR) and Critical Design Review (CDR), and in obtaining expertise in mission equipment subsystems. Properly run, MOAs can create virtual organizations by drawing expertise from other organizations on a just-in-time basis.

Issue: Experienced Personnel. The success of the Predator program aside, there are also potential downside risks to small program offices. As with the DM and the OM, program office individuals should also be carefully selected. Each individual is responsible for a major portion of the program and should be an expert within his or her subject area. Similarly, the composition of the organization must ensure an adequate level of military expertise in order to effectively execute the program according to the desires of the operational user.

Recommendation: The fast pace of the ACTD, coupled with the small size of the program office, magnifies mistakes caused by inexperienced personnel: There is not enough leeway in an ACTD project for people who are new to the acquisition environment. Programs such as the Predator ACTD require seasoned veterans.

Measures of Program Control

Flexibility and creativity were key to the success of the Predator ACTD. Along these lines, the program management team utilized two types of program-control measures that were somewhat different from those used in the formal acquisition process: (1) an emphasis on informal communication and (2) limited CDRL items.

Issue: Emphasis on Informal Communication. Whereas traditional acquisition programs still tend to rely on program controls such as C/SCSC reporting, formal review meetings, and large volumes of documentation, the Predator ACTD did not. On the contrary, the Predator program office used informal daily communication between itself and the contractor, as well as weekly reviews over the phone. Similarly, very little C/SCSC reporting occurred. There appeared to be little utility to the content of those schedule and cost reports that were completed, because, many times, cost and schedule problems had already been discussed and resolved prior to the JPO's receipt of C/SCSC from GA-ASI.

Issue: CDRL Items. The contract between the UAV JPO and GA-ASI required less than 30 CDRL items, which, relative to formal acquisition programs, represents a small number of reports to be required from a contractor. Similar to the goals of acquisition streamlining in the DoD 5000 Series, the Predator ACTD management philosophy was to order as few CDRLs as possible in order to eliminate undesired documentation and to save money.

Although the ACTD achieved both of these goals, it appeared that it may have cut back too much on documentation. For example, the JPO had no information regarding the reliability of the Predator system. From the perspectives of supportability planning and life-cycle cost, it was impossible for management of the Predator ACTD to be capable of making sound, long-term plans. Likewise, there were no formal engineering drawings of the Predator and its subsystems; consequently, it was impossible for the government to procure spare parts from other vendors or to repair the system by using government depots.

Recommendation: We recommend that other ACTDs carefully review the types of CDRLs being requested. As a minimum, the program office should know technical information that will allow it to begin planning for supportability of the system.

Selection of Lead Service

The responsibility of the lead service in an ACTD includes funding, direction, and operational use of the system after the ACTD is completed. As the lead service for the Predator ACTD, the Air Force was also deemed responsible for the training of such operational personnel as the pilot, payload operators, and maintenance technicians. Two specific issues arose from the choice of the Air Force as the lead service in the Predator ACTD: (1) the timing of the lead service decision was too late and (2) the methodology for choosing the Air Force was extremely subjective.

Issue: Timing of Decision. The lead service was designated on December 16, 1995, by the Joint Requirements Oversight Council (JROC)—only seven months before the Predator ACTD was scheduled to end. Prior to this decision, Air Force personnel had not rigorously participated in either the development of the CONOPS or in the demonstration of the Predator. Nor had they provided inputs into the creation of test plans, supportability requirements, or changes of the technical baseline of the system. By many accounts, the Air Force had not been an active participant in the Predator ACTD, yet it was expected to take the reins of the system upon completion. Another problem with the timing of the lead-service choice was that it occurred after USACOM had declared the Predator to have military utility. Needless to say, because the Air Force had not been designated the lead service until after utility had been declared, it was not directly involved in the recommendation. A significant lesson learned from the Predator ACTD is that the designation of lead service for ACTDs must occur early in the process.

Recommendation: Considering all of the activities associated with an ACTD that benefit from the input of the lead service, we recommend that the declaration of lead service occur at the start of the ACTD.

Choosing a lead service early in the program would have provided ample time for operational characteristics to be assessed and requirements to be planned. In theory, the purpose of USACOM as the OM was to represent all services. However, as observed from the Air Force's balking at the system's requirements upon designation as the lead service, it was apparent that the Air Force and USACOM had different ideas of what constituted an "adequate amount" of supportability planning, cost estimating, and technical parameters. If the USAF had been chosen as the lead service earlier in the ACTD, it may have taken greater interest during the operational deployment of the system and, likewise, may have been more proactive in resolving problems.

Issue: Methodology for Selection. The methodology that was used by USACOM to choose the lead service involved a matrix approach, which compared lead-service contenders against a set of criteria that included variables such as operations, manning, training, basing, and logistics. USACOM rated each variable numerically, summed the ratings, and made a recommendation according to which service had the highest total. Ideally, more organizations would have been involved and the ratings would have been made on the basis of quantitative parameters, or metrics. Interestingly, the USACOM's recommendation was not the same as JROC's: USACOM recommended that the Army serve as the lead service; the JROC chose the Air Force.

Recommendation: To avert future conflicts, more-quantitative and more-objective criteria must be stated up front. A standardization of criteria would provide a foundation for an open and objective competition. Possible approaches would involve cost-benefit techniques similar to the current depot-repair–selection process. Results would then be coordinated and approved at the JROC level.

Declaration of Military Utility

The fundamental purpose of an ACTD is to demonstrate the military utility of a system. Echoing the preceding discussion of lead-service selection, two problem areas that arose in demonstrating the military utility of the Predator ACTD were (1) that military utility was declared prior to the designation of the Air Force as the lead service and (2) that a well-defined process of assessing such utility was lacking.

Issue: Timing Relative to Selection of Lead-Service Selection. Although USACOM theoretically represented all uniformed services, it is doubtful that it adequately defined the objectives of concern to the Air Force. Earlier participation by ACC would have also provided USACOM with additional support in overseeing the ACTD and determining the Air Force's perspective on the definition of *utility*.

Recommendation: The lead service, which would have been selected at the start of the ACTD, would define *utility* in conjunction with USACOM or other future lead office or command.

Issue: Methodology for Assessing Utility. The second issue, the lack of a well-defined process for utility assessment, relates to USACOM's attempt to define *military utility* by comparing CONOPS objectives with Predator's accomplishments (see Figure 3.5): All of the key objectives by which utility should have been assessed may not have been captured, because USACOM's assessment was done subjectively and did not include the validation of quantitative requirements, such as MTBF and effective sorties.

Recommendation: Our recommendation for future ACTDs is that DUSD/AT and the Joint Staff determine a policy and process for how military utility should be assessed. To date, no such policy exists. This leads to the question of what types of criteria should be considered in determining utility. Although cost was not considered in the Predator ACTD, it would seem logical that an operational user and lead service consider cost as part of their utility function. Other criteria may include how easily the system can be supported and how well the system can be integrated with other existing weapon systems.

Stability of Funding

Issue: Funding for Duration. The success of the Predator ACTD was partially attributable to the stability of funding for the program throughout its 30-month schedule. This characteristic is necessary for success in formal acquisition programs as well. However, an ACTD's compressed schedule means that minimal time exists for workarounds; unstable funding could cause problems by disrupting the ACTD. In the worst-case scenario, the operational user may lose interest if support is not maintained or if the ACTD schedule is slipped. Whereas formal acquisition programs may be able to adjust their schedules or rescale performance efforts to adjust to decreases in funding, an ACTD schedule would be impossible to condense while simultaneously ensuring program viability. Similarly, the scope of ACTDs admits little adjustment: ACTDs are generally intended to demonstrate a specific type of technology; therefore, anything less than a complete demonstration could result in the warfighter's not understanding the actual utility of the system.

Recommendation: Our recommendation for future ACTDs is that funding stability be maintained throughout the life of the ACTD.

Personnel Requirements

Three issues are associated with the development of appropriate manning requirements for the Predator ACTD: (1) the services' commitment of personnel resources, (2) ensuring that the appropriate personnel skills are required, and (3) the need for expeditious training of all personnel.

Issue: Service Commitment. Although the JPO attempted to solicit support from among the services early in the Predator ACTD, it was not initially successful. Because of the resource constraints on the services, they were hesitant to provide personnel; doing so would have meant that less capability was available for other essential mission areas. Indeed, USACOM made several requests prior to eventually receiving an adequate number of people. This problem was exacerbated by the Air Force's not being designated the lead service until late in the ACTD schedule; an earlier declaration may have focused the personnel issue upon the Air Force as opposed to forcing USACOM and the JPO to draw from all the services.

Recommendation: Our recommendation from the Predator case is that personnel requirements be established early in the ACTD schedule to ensure that the program office and operational sponsor (USACOM in the Predator ACTD) have ample time to assemble enough personnel.

Issue: Uniformity of Skills. Second, having no well-established requirements for personnel skills across the services, such as standardized grade and occupation requirements, meant that the JPO left to the services the discretion for deciding the types of personnel who would be assigned to the ACTD. For example, pilot-operators of the Predator included navigators, fixed-wing pilots, and helicopter pilots. No standards were set for maintenance or support personnel either. Essentially, the services provided whomever they wanted. Needless to say, this posed a challenge because of the differences in type of personnel.

Recommendation: For future ACTDs, a better approach to this problem would be for the program office to define the types of skills necessary for operation of the system.

Issue: Training. Third, it was evident in the Predator ACTD that GA-ASI had significant leverage over the government because military personnel had not been fully qualified, and training was limited for support personnel. Training of pilots to operate the Predator UAV received more emphasis, but relatively little was given to the training of support personnel. This disparity limited the JPO's ability to use government personnel to autonomously support the Predator. Rather, they relied heavily upon GA-ASI for contractor logistics support.

Recommendation: Personnel should be trained as soon as possible. Contractor support may be warranted in the short term. However, to ensure that the system operates effectively, it seems logical that military operators be qualified on the system as soon as possible. Similarly, training should encompass not only operations (for example, pilot or payload operator in the Predator ACTD) but maintenance (e.g., maintenance technicians) as well.

Involvement of OTAs in ACTDs

Whereas formal acquisition programs require a myriad of test-planning exercises and activities such as TEMPs, developmental testing, and operational testing, the ACTD process demands less-formal testing. Two issues arose during the Predator ACTD that can be generalized and applied to other ACTDs as lessons learned: (1) early involvement of the Operational Test Agencies (OTAs) is necessary and (2) testing of the system in an operational setting is beneficial.

Issue: Timing of Involvement. Although DESA and AFOTEC played key roles in assessing the performance of the Predator ACTD, AFOTEC was brought into the ACTD process late. Subsequently, it was required to catch up on a number of technical and programmatic issues. If involved earlier, AFOTEC could have developed demonstration scenarios unique to the Air Force as the lead service, which would have benefited the Predator ACTD. Likewise, AFOTEC could have provided more feedback during the operational-assessment process. Given that AFOTEC will be involved in future OT&E qualification of the Predator system as it makes the transition into the formal acquisition process, up-front inputs by AFOTEC could have potentially alleviated future rework by the program, which would have enabled program managers to identify improvement areas for testing in the formal acquisition process.

Recommendation: Future ACTDs should include OTAs earlier in the process—especially those OTAs that are part of the lead service.

Issue: Benefits of Operational Testing. Although formal testing should not be conducted prior to the transition of the ACTD, much benefit was gained from demonstrating the Predator in the operational environment. For example, deployment of the Predator to Bosnia proved invaluable for several reasons: The contractor received immediate feedback for design consideration, the operational users were able to observe the system at work, and the acquisition managers were able to document potential system deficiencies for future upgrades. Many of these benefits were gained specifically because the Predator was being used in realistic scenarios as opposed to artificial test environments.

Recommendation: We recommend that other ACTDs design their demonstrations, where applicable, around operational scenarios.

ACTD TRANSITION ISSUES

When the Predator ACTD began in late 1993, the intention was not to make a transition to a formal acquisition program but to focus the total attention of the government and contractor team on building the Predator UAV and demonstrating it to operational users for an assessment of military utility. In June 1995, because the Predator was proving itself effective, senior DoD managers began discussions about transition of the Predator to the formal acquisition process. Transition of the Predator UAV from ACTD to acquisition program required that the management team (1) have a plan that included the procurement of additional Predator systems and (2) execute that plan. In this section, we describe the key transition issues for the Predator ACTD, which are summarized in Table 4.3. As in the preceding section, the issues presented here can be applied to other ACTDs as well.

Supportability

Formal acquisition programs require thorough logistics planning, which includes logistics support analysis (LSA), reliability and maintainability studies, and depot maintenance decisions. The ACTD process is less demanding of supportability because people are con-

Table 4.3

ACTD Transition Issues

Subject	Issues
Supportability	• Need for planning • Operational user involvement • Technical orders and data • Residual support
Producibility	• Effect on initial source selection
Program oversight	• OSD involvement • Type of management organization
Funding and affordability	• POM wedge for follow-on work • Need for life-cycle-cost estimate
Operational Requirements Document (ORD)	• Development of a draft ORD • Inclusion of reliability and maintainability goals
Test planning	• Development of an initial DT&E plan • Documenting feedback from operational assessments

cerned first and foremost with the technical aspects of the demonstration, as was management of the Predator ACTD. This is not to say, however, that support of the system should take a backseat to other factors in the ACTD process. It is important to address as many logistics issues as possible as early as possible. Failure to consider system supportability could result in precipitous program-cost growth if significant modifications are required later. Likewise, all parties involved in the ACTD must understand the extent of logistics planning that has been completed or is planned for completion prior to the end of the ACTD, so that decisionmakers are provided with a better estimate of life-cycle costs and program risks that could occur during the formal acquisition process.

Four important supportability issues arose during the Predator ACTD that hampered effective transition of the system: (1) Logistics planning was scarce, (2) maintenance and support personnel had minimal operational involvement, (3) the government did not own any technical orders or maintenance data on the Predator system, and (4) at the conclusion of the ACTD, the government did not analyze the type of maintenance that would be best for support of residual assets.

Issue: Need for Planning. First, it was apparent to us, from the multitude of comments by the DESA and AFOTEC operational assessments, that the JPO spent little time and few resources on anticipating supportability issues. It dealt, instead, with problems as they arose. Even after being informed of supportability problems, the JPO decided, many times, to postpone addressing such issues until the formal acquisition process began—clearly not the best action to take.

Recommendation: Early input into the design of the Predator system can prevent future problems.

Issue: Operational User Involvement. Second, although operational users had substantial input into the operation and technical capabilities of the UAV, maintenance personnel had minimal involvement in the Predator's development. *How* the system would be supported received little attention. For example, the CONOPS never addressed what types of containers would enable the most-effective transportation, how military personnel would fix broken components, or whether parts were reliable. Problems created by the absence of maintenance inputs were exacerbated by the lateness of the Air Force's entry into the ACTD. Given that the Air Force, as the lead service, would eventually be responsible for the maintenance of the system, it should have been involved as early as possible in supportability decisions.

It was also apparent from discussions among USACOM, the JPO, and ACC that each had different concepts of how supportability of the Predator system should occur. Toward the end of the ACTD, the USAF was relatively more active than it had been, eventually relocating a maintainer from ACC to the JPO, a move that should have been made much earlier in the process. The result of the delay is that the USAF may have to support the system as it existed at the end of the ACTD, rather than making significant modifications to the UAV and its support equipment during the formal acquisition process.

Recommendation: Early involvement of the operational user ensures that the system is constructed with the *potential* for growth and flexibility in supportability.

Issue: Technical Orders and Data. Third, the government never requested an adequate amount of logistics information during the ACTD: It did not know the reliability of the Predator system, did not have a list showing the number and quantities of spare parts, and never procured technical orders for operation and maintenance of the system. Although GA-ASI did provide flight manuals for the pilot and payload operators, military maintenance personnel did not have schematics for fixing the Predator and relied on GA-ASI for support of the entire system. Other ACTDs must seriously consider procuring reliability information, spares lists, and, possibly even the development of technical orders for systems that it intends to maintain.

Recommendation: This is not to say that the government must demand all documentation up front, or, for that matter, request that a full-blown LSA be conducted. We recommend that more oversight be given to the logistics planning process, short of requesting extensive amounts of data from the contractor.

Issue: Support of Residual Assets. The fourth issue deals with the future support of residual Predators after the conclusion of the ACTD. As noted, the JPO relied heavily on GA-ASI to maintain the Predator. Instead of using Contractor Logistics Support (CLS) after military utility was declared in fall 1995, it may have behooved the JPO to transition more training and support initiatives to the lead service. Doing so would have required the JPO to conduct cost-benefit trade studies to determine the effectiveness of a CLS as opposed to an Air Force maintenance capability. However, such analysis was not conducted. This, coupled with the fact that the JPO never requested technical orders from the contractor, made it virtually impossible for the Air Force to maintain the system. Consequently, the government is essentially locked into a CLS-type contract with GA-ASI during the residual-support phase.

Recommendation: We recommend that other ACTDs consider the analysis of such support issues earlier in the program to determine whether CLS is desired. If not, they should procure maintenance manuals and reliability data.

Producibility

In an acquisition program, producibility issues are part of the competitive process and source selection from the very start. In an ACTD, the competitive focus of the program is based primarily on technical and schedule issues. During the Predator ACTD, no consideration was given to follow-on production in the initial contract with GA-ASI. Rather, the focus was on the ability of the contractor to build a limited number of systems for determination of military utility. The same systems were also expected to serve as residual assets for USACOM and ACC after the ACTD program was completed.

From the perspective of making the transition to the formal acquisition process, it is obvious that the ability of a contractor to produce assets is a key to the program's longevity. For many ACTDs, the contractors tend to be smaller firms that do not have the industrial capability or personnel resources of other, larger firms. Likewise, their experience with increased production, to the degree that is accomplished in a formal acquisition program, may be extremely limited or altogether nonexistent—a concern for the government if the ACTD transitions to the formal acquisition process, because the contractor may not be able to produce the quantity of systems the government desires. In selecting the contractor for the Predator ACTD, no consideration was given to the ability of the GA-ASI to ramp up production.

Recommendation: To alleviate this concern, we recommend that producibility considerations be recognized during the early stages of the ACTD: Producibility should be considered an evaluation item during the source-selection process. Including this criterion up front will mitigate some of the risks associated with producing the system later on.

Program Oversight

During the Predator ACTD, the JPO had oversight from OSD, as well as its own reporting chain through the Navy. The relationship proved to be beneficial because it provided management recommendations as well as protection from funding instability. Although the ACTD process allows for the use of an oversight panel, no policy at present provides guidance on the type of oversight that should exist after the ACTD is complete. From observing the Predator ACTD, we can point to two oversight-related issues: (1) the amount of OSD involvement and (2) the type of organization that should manage the ACTD during its transition to the formal acquisition process.

Issue: OSD Involvement. In military acquisition, many different organizations are involved in the oversight of a formal acquisition program: OSD; the Service Acquisition Executives (SAEs); systems commands, such as NAVAIR or the Air Force Materiel Command; Program Executive Officers (PEOs); defense agencies; and defense laboratories. Although the focus of ACTDs is different from that of formal acquisition programs, many of the same organizations are involved in managing the demonstration programs as well. For example, OSD played a key role in bringing the services together to manage and assess the utility of the Predator ACTD. Likewise, it provided the initial funding for the ACTD.

After the Predator was completed in July 1996, it was not clear what role OSD played. Possibly because the Predator was a Class II ACTD, which had a well-defined lead service and development organization, more OSD involvement was not required to ensure its viability. However, for Class III ACTDs, in which many programs are involved, it seems logical that OSD take a more hands-on role. If it does not, the program structure could disintegrate, because the needs of the individual services may outweigh the existence of the ACTD.

Recommendation: We recommend that OSD consider continuing mentoring post-ACTD programs until they are well established into the formal acquisition process. This will mitigate the risk of programs' failing during transition owing to lack of interest.

Issue: Type of Management Organization. Second, the structure of the organization that should exist after the ACTD is completed should be identified. The JPO continued to perform acquisition responsibilities for the Predator while the Air Force had the responsibility for the operation of the system and the training of personnel. Since the end of the ACTD, there has been some indication that the Air Force may eventually take the lead for acquisition responsibilities as well.

The setup between the JPO and the USAF has appeared to work well to date; however, the complexity of Class III ACTDs presents a different type of concern. Class III ACTDs, such as the Counter-proliferation and the Rapid Force Projection Initiative, are not managed by such joint-service organizations as the UAV JPO, although the ACTD incorporates programs from more than one service. Should programs like these be managed by lead services, a joint program office, or a "super" organization such as DARO, the Ballistic Missile Defense Organization (BMDO), or the Defense Special Weapons Agency (DSWA)? Each of these latter organizations was created for a specific purpose that may not fit the purpose of the ACTD. Similarly, formation of new "super" organizations to manage Class III ACTDs may be negatively viewed as a way to increase the number of organizations within the DoD.

Recommendation: We recommend that USD(A&T) establish a policy for how ACTDs are to be managed after their completion.

Funding and Affordability

The Predator ACTD encountered two funding and affordability issues that also could affect the transition effectiveness of other ACTDs: (1) the need for a life-cycle-cost estimate and (2) the use of a program objective memorandum (POM) funding wedge to bridge potential funding gaps.

Issue: Life-Cycle-Cost Estimate. With respect to the first issue, it did not appear that the UAV JPO was concerned about the overall life-cycle cost of the Predator system. Throughout the ACTD, management was concerned about the unit flyaway cost of the Predator UAV but did not consider other costs incurred for supportability. Although the fast pace and short-term focus of the ACTD do not necessarily encourage or provide incentives for a program manager to consider long-term effects, supportability and reliability of a system are known to make up a significant portion of the total LCC.

Recommendation: We recommend that, for future ACTDs, the government conduct an LCC analysis as part of the transition planning process. This will ensure that DoD leaders are aware of the expected costs of a system and will not be surprised later in the formal acquisition process. Similarly, if the LCC appears prohibitive, the government would benefit from having this information before the transition and may desire to cancel or redesign the system by the use of cost trade studies.

Issue: POM Wedge for Follow-On Work. In the Predator ACTD, management ensured funding for support of residual assets at the end of the demonstration. Likewise, they began to plan for funding for the transition to the formal acquisition process. If they had not initiated such planning, it is highly likely that time delays caused by POM actions could have cancelled benefits derived from the ACTD.

Recommendation: We recommend that transition funding requirements be adequately planned for and budgeted prior to the end of the ACTD, possibly in the form of a funding wedge in the POM.

Operational Requirements Document

The specifications of a formal acquisition program are defined by its Operational Requirements Document (ORD), which also quantifies the expected system performance. For example, an aircraft ORD would specify required flight parameters such as speed, altitude, and endurance. Besides serving as the vision for the program, the ORD also is used during Initial Operational Test and Evaluation (IOT&E) to assess how well the system meets the needs of the warfighter. Compare this to the ACTD process, in which an ORD is not required. With regard to an ORD in the Predator ACTD, two key issues arose: (1) the potential for use of a draft ORD and (2) the necessity for inclusion of reliability and maintainability goals in the ORD.

Issue: Development of a Draft ORD. The closest document the Predator had to an ORD was its CONOPS, which served as the framework for the program. It defined operational characteristics of the Predator, and it described some supportability aspects of the program; however, it never fulfilled the entire role of an ORD. Instead, the DM and the OM waited until the end of the ACTD to begin developing its requirements document. Given that the Air Force was brought in late to the program, it never gave the type of inputs into the ORD that it thought were needed. Instead, upon completion of the ACTD, the USAF viewed preparation of a Predator ORD as a backfilling exercise: The ORD was written to describe the existing Predator system rather than to specify what was desired by the operational user. Needless to say, there was much consternation among the JPO, USACOM, and ACC on this point.

Recommendation: To resolve this type of dilemma for future ACTDs, we recommend that the ORD be an iteratively defined, living document in the sense that it is continuously refined and considers activities and lessons learned throughout the entire life of the demonstration program. Unlike the Predator, for which the ACC was asked to approve a document it had not actively participated in developing, the ORD should be based on the needs of the warfighter. This would facilitate warfighters' having greater input into the process early on as well as the nomination of a lead service that could accomplish the drafting of the document. Instead of the complete ORD that is used in the formal acquisition process, a draft ORD could be written in more-general terms during the ACTD. By the time the ACTD was completed, the ORD would have been fully collaborated upon by developer, user, and lead service and would likewise provide great continuity as the program transitions into the formal acquisition process.

Issue: Inclusion of Reliability and Maintainability Goals Up Front. Along with operational requirements, supportability and reliability requirements must be stated in the early stages the ACTD. This is not to say that *all* reliability parameters must be defined at the start of the ACTD but, rather, that the opportunity should exist for maintenance and support personnel to provide their inputs into the process. If the ACTD is a joint-service program like Predator, then all of the services should designate representatives to voice their opinion of supportability requirements.

Recommendation: Given that different services have different needs, we recommend that the DM and the OM balance supportability needs against cost, schedule, and technical performance. Incorporating ideas up front will mitigate future cost growth from potential changes in requirements.

Test Planning

As seen in the section on demonstration issues, OTAs played an important role in the assessment of the Predator ACTD. Similarly, two issues relate to test activities that are important for the effective transitioning of an ACTD to the formal acquisition process: (1) the development of an initial DT&E plan and (2) the documentation of feedback from operational assessments.

Issue: Development of an Initial DT&E Plan. Although not accomplished in the Predator ACTD, the government should consider developing a DT&E plan prior to transitioning an ACTD to the formal acquisition process. Doing so would save time during the acquisition phase. Similarly, by forcing the program to start planning for DT&E, management may be more likely to document its lessons learned from the test area for future use.

Recommendation: We recommend that, before the transition process begins, a plan be developed to define the types of test documentation that will be required later. One discovery made during this research was that most organizations thought that documentation was not required because the Predator was an ACTD. Thus, organizations decided not to define how they would complete documents such as TEMPs until late in the ACTD and early in the formal acquisition process. Planning in the near-term portion of the program, during the ACTD phase, could alleviate future schedule, program, or cost problems during the formal acquisition process. The depth of planning should be conditional upon the expectation of the probability of success of the program.

Issue: Documenting Feedback from Operational Assessments. The second issue regards documenting formal lessons learned from the OAs. In reviewing the Predator OAs written by DESA and AFOTEC, we became aware that problems arose in many areas during the ACTD. Most of the problems involved supportability, training, and maintenance. Specifically, several comments related to the lack of spare parts, inadequacy of personnel levels, and shortages of key equipment items. These comments were used by the JPO during the ACTD process. Other comments could be used similarly after the Predator has transitioned to the formal acquisition process.

Recommendation: We recommend that other ACTDs also have organized feedback processes to ensure that follow-on work will be of even greater benefit.

How Much Planning Is Enough?

As a conclusion to this section, we need to ask, How much planning is enough? It depends. Given the necessity for expediency, limited funding, and the goal of demonstrating military utility, it is impossible to dictate exactly how much planning should occur for a given ACTD and when. However, this is not to say that general rules cannot be applied. As evidenced by this section, several types of planning must occur to ensure a proper transition to the formal acquisition process: supportability, funding, test, producibility, organization structure, and the drafting of an ORD. Although ACTDs neither require nor can facilitate extremely detailed planning for every topic, this report has highlighted that the nonexistence of any planning could potentially cost a program significant resources in the long run.

Certainty that an ACTD will transition to the formal acquisition process is the watchword for planning. As the certainty of transition increases, more planning should be conducted during the ACTD. The converse also holds true: Where certainty of transition decreases, less planning should occur. Intuitively, if Predator had been earmarked for definite transition to an acquisition program early in the ACTD, more planning should have been accomplished. However, this would probably have required more up-front funds and additional personnel.

We recommend that the DoD continue to pursue the use of transition integrated product teams, as it plans to do in the future. Although every ACTD should not necessarily make the transition into the formal acquisition process immediately, the TIPT must assume a positive projection. That is, the TIPTs must assume that the program will be successful during the ACTD phase and will ultimately transition. Having TIPTs with this type of vision will help facilitate the transition of the ACTD into a formal acquisition program with minimal schedule and program problems.

COMPARISON OF THE PREDATOR ACTD WITH A FORMAL ACQUISITION PROGRAM

The preceding two sections highlight issues regarding the demonstration and transition of the Predator ACTD to the formal acquisition process. An important outcome of the discussion was the comparison of the ACTD process and the DoD 5000 Series. It was evident throughout the analysis that there were several differences between an ACTD like the Predator and a formal acquisition program like an F-22, F/A-18, or RAH-66. Most of the difference was due to three key variables: (1) the depth of planning accomplished, (2) the formality of processes, and (3) the amount of documentation required. For comparison, Table 4.4 summarizes the attributes of the Predator ACTD and those of a typical formal acquisition program, discussed in this chapter.

First and foremost, the two processes have markedly different goals. Whereas the goal of the Predator ACTD was to *demonstrate* the military utility of a system, the objective of the formal acquisition process is to *produce* systems. Accordingly, the acquisition process emphasizes intense planning to ensure that a program does not fail while in its development stage or while in use by the warfighter. Most program managers would agree that planning is critical to successful program execution and avoidance of problems during and after system production. Examples of in-depth planning performed in an acquisition program, but not present in the Predator ACTD, include the following: supportability analysis, life-cycle costing, procurement strategies, producibility, and formal risk-management techniques.

The second difference was seen in the formality and execution of processes. For an ACTD like Predator, few formal processes existed. Rather, the DM and the OM had great flexibility in how they conducted the management of the ACTD. In a formal acquisition program, however, management processes are more rigidly defined. Although there have been recent attempts at streamlining the acquisition process, by its very nature, the DoD 5000 Series provides structure to the procurement of weapon systems. Similarly, the federal acquisition regulations (FARs) lay the foundation for contractual issues and serve as the legal framework for business decisions. Other formal processes that exist in a formal acquisition program but that are not required by an ACTD include the following: the development and use of an Operational Requirements Document, adherence to an acquisition program baseline, the formal use of integrated product teams, required management control documents, and the employment of a formal testing program.

Table 4.4

Comparison of the Predator ACTD with a Formal Acquisition Program

Item	Present in the Predator ACTD?	Present in a Formal Acquisition Program?
Operational Requirements Document (ORD)	One-page statement from USD(A&T)	Yes
Management plan	Yes (management plan)	Yes (acquisition program baseline)
Clear lines of authority and responsibility	Yes	Yes
Single responsible official for managing the program (government/contractor)	Yes/yes	Yes/yes
Formal use of integrated product teams (IPTs)	No	Yes
Management control documents	Limited (C/SCSC)	Extensive (C/SCSC)
Open communication	Yes	Yes
Formal program reviews	Limited/infrequent	Extensive/regularly scheduled
Supportability issues addressed	No	Yes
Maintenance concept type	Contractor-furnished throughout ACTD	Combination of government/contractor
Testing concept/TEMP (IOT&E)	No (TEMP, CONOPS/user demo, independent operational assessment)	Yes (formal TEMP, independent IOT&E)
Acquisition program documentation	Minimum	Maximum
Life-cycle cost/affordability/CAIV	No	Yes
Procurement strategy for life cycle	No	Yes
Producibility considered	No	Yes
Formal risk-management program	No	Yes

Table 4.4—continued

Item	Present in the Predator ACTD?	Present in a Formal Acquisition Program?
User involvement	Yes—through actual operation	Yes—through user representative
User assessments	Military utility determined by operational command	Only accomplished through separate operational testing
Time frame	Accelerated, short time periods; usually 2–4 years	Extensive, drawn-out; sometimes 6–10 years
Exit criteria	No	Yes

The final difference between an ACTD and a formal acquisition program is the amount of documentation that is required. For the Predator, C/SCSC reporting was limited, only 30 CDRL items were requested from GA-ASI, and the JPO required minimal acquisition program documentation. By contrast, a formal acquisition program makes extensive use of C/SCSC reporting, tasks such as LSA and engineering require many CDRL items, and program documentation is voluminous. Over the past five years, attempts have been made to reduce the amount of documentation that is requested by a formal acquisition program, but the government has been relatively slow to change on this point.

Chapter Five

CONCLUSIONS

During the past decade, the acquisition community has experienced great change as the military has been faced with significant constraints on its ability to procure weapon systems. To maintain a robust posture in the face of reductions in procurement funding, the DoD has concentrated on increasing both the effectiveness and efficiency of the existing acquisition framework. Recent examples include the use of streamlining of acquisition business processes, process improvement teams, and the Advanced Concept Technology Demonstration. The idea for ACTDs was generated by senior DoD leaders in 1993 because of their perception that the formal acquisition process was inefficient in demonstrating new technology to warfighters. By its very nature, an ACTD program is expected to be an operational demonstration to assess the military utility of a system. Acceptance or rejection of the ACTD is based on the warfighter's evaluation of such utility. During the same time that the ACTD process was formulated, the Predator UAV was selected as the first program to demonstrate the ACTD idea.

Although the process for approval and conducting ACTDs was being finalized in 1994, limited thought was given to how ACTDs would make the transition to the formal acquisition process upon their completion. Discussion focused on proper entry points in the formal acquisition process and guidelines for transition preparation. Given the fast pace of ACTDs, the lack of formal acquisition rules, and the limited operational capability of the systems, questions abounded on how to conduct and successfully characterize an effective transition process. This report has presented our interpretation of the Predator ACTD and the demonstration and transition issues that arose during our analysis of the program. The ultimate goal was to generalize issues for their application to other ACTDs. Table 5.1 summarizes those recommendations we derived from our analysis of the Predator ACTD that can be applied to other ACTDs.

For the most part, methods for managing ACTDs are new within the DoD. They represent a major cultural change over how past systems have been developed and demonstrated in the formal acquisition process. Until recently, business operations in the acquisition environment had focused on life-cycle acquisition and support. Consequently, most individuals within the acquisition system are accustomed to using the following DoD 5000 methods for managing

Table 5.1

Recommendations from Analysis of the Predator ACTD

- Given the necessarily fast pace of the ACTD process, confident, effective, and innovative individuals are critical to the success of a program.

- The lead service must be selected early in the ACTD process to ensure that (1) proper test and logistics planning occurs, (2) operational requirements are fleshed out, and (3) warfighters have commitment to the system to ensure its longevity and success.

- An ACTD needs to be managed significantly differently than are formal acquisition programs, because of the (1) fast-paced program schedule, (2) small number of program office personnel, and (3) limited guidance on how to perform the acquisition of the system.

- Test agencies such as DESA and AFOTEC made beneficial suggestions; their involvement should be considered with future ACTDs.

- The lead-service organization should develop a draft Operational Requirements Document during the ACTD process. The process of writing and constantly updating the ORD will (1) resolve any misunderstanding of requirements among developers and warfighters, (2) help define quantitative system specifications, and (3) facilitate transition of the ACTD to the acquisition process.

- Early in their schedule, ACTDs should consider more in-depth planning than was done on the Predator. Planning discussions must involve operational users, lead-service personnel, and acquisition experts who can assess functional areas such as test, logistics, engineering, and affordability. Such planning is especially important if a strong probability exists that the ACTD will make the transition to the formal acquisition process upon its completion.

programs: (1) avoidance of past mistakes, (2) a focus on risk mitigation, and (3) a strict adherence to formal processes. In the past several years, however, revisions to the DoD 5000 Series have facilitated streamlining of acquisition business processes and have encouraged people to think about more-creative and more-effective solutions to problems. Acquisition-reform initiatives have concentrated on improving processes to procure systems faster, more cost-effectively, and with the use of more-commercial practices and commercial off-the-shelf items. Although of great long-term benefit to the DoD, these changes have not been easy to implement culturally by policymakers because of the paradigms held by stakeholders of the formal acquisition process.

From the findings of and lessons learned in our research, we can recognize the eventual connectivity between ACTDs and DoD 5000 requirements. Although many of the issues focus upon more planning, closer coordination among participants, and greater resources (for example, more people, more funding for LCC and cost estimates), this is not meant to propose that the methods for managing ACTD programs should evolve in scope or detail as do those associated with DoD 5000 programs. On the contrary, the utility of the ACTD process lies in its ability to expediently demonstrate new technologies to operational users. As highlighted in Chapter Four, ACTDs are different from formal acquisition programs in three respects: (1) the depth of planning accomplished, (2) the formality of processes, and (3) the amount of documentation required. We expect that recommendations from this study will aid in making the ACTD process a more effective and efficient one by recognizing that every ACTD is unique and that the content of the program must be tailored to best fit the objectives of the program.

BIBLIOGRAPHY

Aerospace Daily, July 21, 1995, pp. 102–104.

"After 120 Days . . . Predator Returns from Balkan Deployment; Will Seek De-Icing System," *Inside the Air Force,* October 27, 1995, p. 5.

Air Force Operational Test and Evaluation Center (AFOTEC), *MAE UAV (Predator) Operational Assessment Updated Report,* Kirtland AFB, N.M., June 24, 1996.

———, *Policy for Advanced Concept Technology Demonstration,* Kirtland AFB, N.M., HQ AFOTEC/CC, Policy Letter 96-02, April 5, 1996.

Air Force Times, August 26, 1996.

Clifford, B., J. Boatman, and M. Hewish, "UAV Development: The Art of Compromise," *International Defense Review,* May 1993, pp. 377–383.

Curtis, I. G., "UAVs, Growing in Numbers, Finally Become Militarily, Politically and Industrially Attractive," *Defense & Foreign Affairs Strategic Policy,* August 31, 1994, p. 10.

Defense Airborne Reconnaissance Office (DARO), *UAV Annual Report for 1994–1995,* DARO Homepage located at **http://www.acq.osd.mil/daro/uav/.**

Defense Evaluation Support Activity (DESA), *Medium Altitude Endurance (MAE) Unmanned Aerial Vehicle (UAV) Advanced*

Concept Technology Demonstration (ACTD) Recommendations History, August 2, 1996.

————, *Medium Altitude Endurance (MAE) Unmanned Aerial Vehicle (UAV) Advanced Concept Technology Demonstration (ACTD) Recommendations History,* August 2, 1996.

————, *Memorandum of Agreement Between the Defense Evaluation Support Activity and the Air Force Operational Test and Evaluation Center,* 1995.

————, "Overview Briefing," August 1996.

Deputy Under Secretary of Defense for Advanced Technology (DUSD/AT) Larry Lynn, "Tactical Endurance UAV Program," memo to the Assistant Secretary of the Navy for Research, Development & Acquisition, November 17, 1993.

"Deutch Memo"—see Under Secretary of Defense, 1993.

DUSD/AT, "Advanced Concept Technology Demonstrations," briefing, April 17, 1996.

————, "Tactical Endurance Unmanned Aerial Vehicle (UAV) Program," memo to the ASN(RD&A), November 17, 1993.

"DoD, US Customs Service Reject Counterdrug Mission for Predator UAV," *Inside the Air Force,* May 31, 1996, p. 14.

Evers, S., "Big Changes in Store for DoD Intelligence Collection," *Aerospace Daily,* July 21, 1995, p. 103.

————, "GNAT-750 May Raise Profile of UAVs," *Aviation Week & Space Technology,* February 7, 1994, pp. 54–55.

Forecast International/DMS Market Intelligence Report, December 1991.

Fulghum, D. A., "Imagery from Bosnia Expected to Improve," *Aviation Week & Space Technology,* July 24, 1995, pp. 20–21.

————, "New UAV Force Forms at Nellis," *Aviation Week & Space Technology,* July 31, 1995, pp. 21–24.

————, "Tier 2 UAV Aborts First Test Flight," *Aviation Week & Space Technology*, July 11, 1994, p. 22.

————, "USAF Stresses UAVs for Recon," *Aviation Week & Space Technology*, September 27, 1993, p. 44.

Fulghum, D. A., and J. D. Morrocco, "US Readies Predator for Missions in Bosnia," *Aviation Week & Space Technology*, June 5, 1995, p. 22.

————, "U.S. Military to Boost Tactical Recon in '95," *Aviation Week & Space Technology*, January 9, 1995, p. 22.

General Atomics Homepage, located at **http://www.ga.com/**.

"General Atomics to Roll Out Predator UAV," *Aerospace Daily*, August 31, 1994, p. 342.

Goodman, G. W., "Flying High: Air Force Finally Embraces Unmanned Air Vehicles," *Armed Forces Journal International*, October 1995, p. 18.

Inside the Air Force, March 15, 1996, p. 8.

Inside the Pentagon, April 25, 1996, p. 8.

Johnson, Robert V., and John Birkler, *Three Programs and Ten Criteria: Evaluating and Improving Acquisition Program Management and Oversight Processes Within the Department of Defense*, Santa Monica, Calif.: RAND, MR-758-OSD, 1996.

Leibstone, M., "US Unmanned Air Vehicles," *Military Technology*, September 1992, p. 29.

"Lesson-Filled First Flight of Tier II Lasts Only 20 Seconds," *Aerospace Daily*, July 6, 1994, pp. 19A–19B.

Lovece, J. A., "Big Plans, High Hurdles for UAV Joint Program Office," *Armed Forces Journal International*, July 1990, p. 48.

————, "US Military Services Finally Embrace UAVs . . . Just As Procurement Funds Dwindle," *Armed Forces Journal International*, July 1993, p. 21.

Military Technology, October 1991, p. 19.

"On Fogleman's Watch," *Aerospace Daily*, June 19, 1995, p. 435.

Owens, William A., Admiral, Vice Chairman of the Joint Chiefs of Staff, JROCM 151-95, memo to the Honorable William J. Perry, December 16, 1995.

"Perry Describes Bosnia 'Intelligence Cell'," *Aerospace Daily*, June 7, 1995, p. 373.

"Perry to Pitch Predator for Intelligence Role in Bosnia," *Aerospace Daily*, June 6, 1995, p. 365.

Perry, William J., memo to the Joint Chiefs of Staff, April 9, 1996.

"Practically Perfect Predator," *Inside the Air Force*, August 23, 1996, p. 1.

"Predator Crashes Destroy Ku-Band Vehicle," *Aerospace Daily*, August 16, 1995, p. 244.

"Predator for Bosnia Overflights," *Flight International*, July 5–11, 1995, p. 16.

"Predator in Roving Sands," *Interavia*, June 1995, p. 74.

"Predator Makes First Flight from Ft. Huachuca," *Aerospace Daily*, October 28, 1994, p. 151.

"Predator to Go to Bosnia Next Month," *Aerospace Daily*, June 9, 1995, p. 387.

"Predator UAV Being Sent to Albania," *Aerospace Daily*, June 27, 1995, p. 485.

"Predator UAV Ready for Overseas Operations," *Aerospace Daily*, June 5, 1995, p. 357.

"Predator UAV Tests New Ku-band Satcom Link," *Aerospace Daily*, June 5, 1995, p. 360.

"Predator UAV to Be Used in Bosnia, but Without SAR and De-Icing System," *Inside the Air Force*, December 15, 1995, pp. 1–2.

"Shortage of UAV Pilots Prompts Air Force to Be Creative in Filling Gap," *Inside the Air Force*, March 15, 1996, pp. 7–8.

Sommer, G., et al., *The Global Hawk Unmanned Aerial Vehicle Acquisition Process: A Summary of Phase 1 Experience*, Santa Monica, Calif.: RAND, MR-809-DARPA, 1997.

Starr, B., "Two Predator UAVs Lost in Missions Over Bosnia," *Jane's Defence Weekly*, August 26, 1995, p. 8.

Terino, J., "UAVs: A Defense Growth Area," *National Defense*, October 1992, pp. 13–14.

"Tier II UAV Sets Endurance Record," *Aerospace Daily*, January 24, 1995, p. 109.

Under Secretary of Defense John M. Deutch, "Endurance Unmanned Aerial Vehicle (UAV) Program," memo to the Assistant Secretary of the Navy for Research, Development & Acquisition, July 12, 1993.

Under Secretary of Defense for Acquisition and Technology [USD(A&T)], *Advanced Concept Technology Demonstrations Master Plan*, Washington, D.C., August 1996.

———, *Defense Airborne Reconnaissance Office (DARO)*, Washington, D.C.: DoD Directive 5134.11, April 5, 1995.

———, "Policy on Cost-Performance Trade-Offs," memo, July 19, 1995.

———, "Reducing Life Cycle Costs for New and Fielded Systems," memo, December 4, 1995.

Under Secretary of Defense for Acquisition and Technology and the Joint Chiefs of Staff, *ACTD Master Plan*, April 1995.

United States Atlantic Command (USACOM), *Medium Altitude Endurance ACTD Management Plan*, Norfolk, Va., October 1994.

———, "MAE UAV Manning Request," memo to Operational Users and Military Services, March 24, 1995.

———, *Military Utility Assessment for the MAE UAV ACTD*, Norfolk, Va., May 1996.

"USACOM Recommends DoD Acquire 45 Predator Unmanned Aerial Vehicles," *Inside the Air Force*, November 24, 1995, pp. 10–11.

U.S. Department of Defense (DoD), *Defense Airborne Reconnaissance Office (DARO)*, DODD 5134.11, April 5, 1995.

——, *Defense Acquisition*, DODD 5000.1, March 15, 1996.

——, *Mandatory Procedures for Major Defense Acquisition Programs (MDAPs) and Major Automated Information System (MAIS) Acquisition Programs*, DoD Regulation 5000.2-R, December 13, 1996.

——, *Unmanned Aerial Vehicles 1994 Master Plan*, Washington, D.C., May 1994.

U.S. Navy, Naval Air Systems Command, *Operating Agreement Between the Commander, Naval Air Systems Command and the Naval Air Systems Command and the Naval Aviation Program Executive Officers*, Washington, D.C., August 1990.

Unmanned Aerial Vehicle Joint Project Office (UAV JPO), "Tactical Endurance UAV Activity Report," briefing, Washington, D.C., February 18, 1994.

——, "Briefing," Washington, D.C., June 26, 1995.

——, "MAE Project Briefing," Washington, D.C., January 18, 1994.

——, *MAE UAV CONOPS*, Washington, D.C., September 1995.

——, *Medium Altitude Endurance UAV ACTD Management Plan*, Washington, D.C., October 1994.

——, *Monthly MAE UAV PM (DM) to PEO Report*, December 15, 1995.

——, "Predator: MAE IPT Brief," Washington, D.C., June 26, 1995.

——, "Predator System," briefing, Washington, D.C., March 1996.

——, "September 1995 Program Summary Briefing," Washington, D.C.